"William Barclay .... gives clear advice on how bes................................ings came into being and .... ture, and explains the signi.................................."—*Christianity Today*

"This informative little book will make the Bible one of the most exciting challenges life can offer."—*Interpreter*

"Helpful guides for conducting a Bible study. Especially good for the young Christian."—*Christianity Today*

"Barclay is incapable of boring; he is a joyous Christian and his sense of fun shines through his writings."—Clift Rodgers Library

"Fascinating and informative reading."—*Crossroads*

introducing the Bible

William Barclay

ABINGDON

Nashville

INTRODUCING THE BIBLE
A Festival Book

First published 1972 by the Bible Reading Fellowship and
the International Bible Reading Association.

Festival edition published by
Abingdon, February, 1979

Second Printing 1980

ISBN 0-687-19488-1

The Aids to Reading on page 143 is an
abridgement designed for U.S. readers.

MANUFACTURED IN U.S.A.

Contents

Prayers for Bible Study

It was the prayer of the psalmist:
>   Open my eyes, that I may behold
>   wondrous things out of thy law (Psalm 119:18).

O God, our Father,
   Open our eyes and enlighten our minds,
      as we study your word.
So grant that
   our minds may know your truth,
   and our hearts may feel your love;
And then confirm and strengthen our wills,
   that we may go out to live what we have learned:
      through Jesus Christ our Lord, Amen.

O God,
   Help us to study your word,
      not only to know about our blessed Lord,
         but also to know him;
      not only to learn about him,
         but also to encounter him;
      not only to grow in knowledge,
         but also to increase in love;
      not only to love him with our hearts,
         but also to obey him with our lives;
   So that knowing him, loving him, and obeying him,
   we too may say: For me to live is Christ.
      This we ask for your love's sake. Amen.

O God,
   as we study your word,
   grant us persistence,
      that we may not cease from study,
         until we find its meaning.
   Take from us the prejudice,
      which would shut our eyes to the truth.
   Never let us love systems
      more than we love you.
And then give us the humility which will accept and obey

what you say to us and what you tell us to do:
     through Jesus Christ our Lord. Amen.

O God, our Father,
  as we read your word,
    humble us at the sight of your holiness,
      and then comfort us with the memory of your mercy.
    Humiliate us with the realization of our sinfulness,
      and then uplift us at the sight of your love.
              Help us in your word
              to know our sin
              and to find our Savior:
     through Jesus Christ our Lord. Amen.

O God, our Father,
  help us in the study of your word to find
    guidance for our problems,
    strength for our temptations;
    power for our tasks;
    comfort for our sorrows;
    your fellowship for our loneliness.
  When we are lazy and lethargic,
    let your word stimulate us to thought and to action.
  When we are restless and distracted,
    let your word calm our troubled hearts
    with the peace that passes understanding.

In the study of your word, open your hand
and satisfy our every need:
     through Jesus Christ our Lord. Amen.

Preface

My first word must be a word of gratitude to the Bible Reading Fellowship and to the International Bible Reading Association for giving me the privilege and the responsibility of writing this book. I have been teaching the Bible for thirteen years in a parish and for twenty-five years in a university, and I am grateful for the opportunity to set down what I believe it to be, and to describe something of the techniques for the study of it.

We are living in a time particularly favorable for Bible study. Never were there more and better aids for that study. For long enough it was a jibe that unintelligibility was the stock in trade of the theologian; and it was true that many theologians wrote looking over their shoulder at other professional theologians. But nowadays there is a new desire to communicate theology, not to the expert theologian, but to the ordinary person. There is more desire for communication now than for many a long day.

Further, and even more important, there is today a willingness to sit down and to study together which is a new thing. Today we can find Protestant and Roman Catholic sitting down together to study the Bible. Today we find a new sympathy between the conservative and the liberal, between the fundamentalist and the radical. It is not that either is willing to abandon his stance and his beliefs, but it is that both are willing to sit down together and talk, even if they do not agree with each other; and, when they do talk, it sometimes happens that they discover that they are not so far apart as once they thought they were. Here is a new situation with a very great potential.

Augustine Birrell used to say that every student should be compelled to read books with the point of which he is in complete disagreement. In Bible study a very mixed group, with widely varying points of view, is much better than a holy huddle of like-minded people. Disagreement can be the way to new discovery and is always a stimulus to thought, for we can never be sure of any position until we have defended it from attack.

Another new attitude is that people have come to see that the Bible is a book, not only to be read, but also to be studied. The old system in which a person read a chapter a day, and just read it, will no longer do. The old battle-cry that the Bible is its own best interpreter is no longer acceptable. The Bible is a difficult book, written in different languages, coming from a different civilization, talking about difficult things, and every aid to study must be brought to it. The Bible is like all great books—the more we bring to it, the more we will get out of it.

In this book I do not wish to persuade people to think as I do; I only wish to make them think. It is my prayer and my hope that this book will enable people to understand the Bible better, to love it more, and in it to see Jesus Christ more clearly.

WILLIAM BARCLAY

Glasgow University

Chapter 1
The Ancient Book

The first chapter of the Westminster Confession of Faith is entitled *Of the Holy Scripture*. Right at the beginning of that document basic to the Church of Scotland it is laid down that the books of the Bible "are given by inspiration of God, to be the rule of faith and life." The Confession goes on to say that the authority of Scripture "depends wholly upon God," and that therefore it is "the word of God." We are then told that "the whole counsel of God, concerning all things necessary for his own glory, man's salvation, faith and life, is either expressly set down in Scripture, or by good and necessary consequence may be deduced from Scripture; unto which nothing at any time is to be added, whether by new revelations of the Spirit, or traditions of men." And in all the controversies of religion the Scriptures are to be the final court of appeal.

Such then is the position that is given to the Bible. At first sight it is an extraordinary position. The earliest parts of the Bible were written almost three thousand years ago; there is no part of the Bible which is less than eighteen hundred years old; and yet the church accepts this ancient book as having final and binding authority.

In one sense the position is unique. True, there are many ancient text-books still extant, but they are not accepted as final and binding. The doctors do not dictate their treatment by Galen and Hippocrates; the architects do not use the work of Vitruvius as their authority; the farmers do not follow the advice of Varro in their agricultural practice; the astronomers do not follow the astronomy of Ptolemy. To this day these books are read, but they are read as stages on the way, not the end; they are read for their interest, not for their authority. But the Bible, in its earlier parts older than any of them, is still for the Christian the supreme rule of faith and life.

In another sense we do have parallels to this. So long as men read poetry, they will read Homer; so long as men study philosophy, they will read Plato and Aristotle; so long as men are interested in the ethics of the good life, they will read Epictetus and Marcus Aurelius; so long as men love beauty, they will study the statues of Praxiteles. That a thing is old does not necessarily make it irrelevant; many of the oldest things are among the most precious possessions of mankind. But even in these cases there is no claim to the absolute authority to which the Bible lays claim; there is no claim, as the Westminster Confession claims for the Bible, that to this there is nothing left to add. What then is so special about this book?

1. The Bible has in it a sheer beauty which makes it, apart from anything else, an immortal work of literature. We have only to listen to it even in short passages to be moved to the heart with the magic of its words; and this is especially so in the Authorized Version.

> Many waters cannot quench love, neither can the floods drown it: if a man would give all the substance of his house for love, it would be utterly contemned. (Song of Solomon 8:7)
>
> Saul and Jonathan were lovely and pleasant in their lives, and in their death they were not divided. (2 Samuel 1:23)
>
> O my son Absalom, my son, my son Absalom! would God I had died for thee, O Absalom, my son, my son! (2 Samuel 18:33)
>
> Comfort ye, comfort ye my people, saith your God. Speak ye comfortably to Jerusalem, and cry unto her, that her warfare is accomplished, that her iniquity is pardoned. (Isaiah 40:1, 2)
>
> They shall hunger no more, neither thirst any more; neither shall the sun light on them, nor any heat. For the Lamb which is in the midst of the throne shall feed them, and shall lead them unto living fountains of waters: and God shall wipe away all tears from their eyes. (Revelation 7:16, 17)

It would be easy to fill half this book with such passages. Every man will have the passages and the verses which are fixed immovably and forever in his memory, with their inescapable beauty.

If on no other grounds than beauty, the Bible has unanswerable rights to greatness. Coleridge said that constant study of the Bible will keep anyone from being vulgar in point of style. Whatever a man's religious beliefs may be, and even if he has none, no man can claim to be fully educated unless he has read this monument of English prose.

The Greek Longinus wrote one of the great books on literary criticism, and called it *On the Sublime.* For him sublimity was the supreme quality in any writer. When a coin is dropped it gives out a ring, and from that ring you can tell at once whether it is true or base metal, and Longinus said, in a great phrase, that sublimity is the ring of a great soul. And there is no book in the world which has this quality of sublimity as the Bible has.

Undoubtedly, the Bible has the title to greatness for its sheer beauty. But at least to some extent this would mean that the Bible belongs to the luxuries rather than to the basic necessities of life. We must look for more than beauty to explain its claim to its unique place.

2. The Bible is an indispensable history book. The Bible is written against the background of the world movements of the great empires of the Middle East—Egypt, Assyria, Babylonia, Persia, Greece, Rome. Our knowledge of the history of the Middle East would be very considerably lessened without the Bible.

It is quite true that the Jewish idea of history was not that of the professional historian. The one test of any figure in biblical history was his obedience or his disobedience to God. So it is said of Asa that he did that which was right in the eyes of the Lord (1 Kings 15:11), and it is said of Jehoram that he did what was evil in the sight of the Lord (2 Kings 3:2). Omri of Samaria is dismissed in a few lines; he did what was evil in the sight of the Lord (1 Kings 16:25-28); and yet we know from nonbiblical sources that politically Omri was one of the most important of all the kings. The biblical historian will spend more time on the stories of Elijah and Elisha than on the background of world-shaking events. Ahab's conduct in regard to Naboth's vineyard gets a whole chapter to itself (1 Kings 21). All this is true, but without the historians and the prophets of the Old Testament our knowledge of Middle East history would be seriously curtailed. As a history book the Bible occupies a very important place.

But again this is not enough. It is not only time with which the Bible is concerned; it is also eternity. We must look further for the reason of its uniqueness.

3. From the point of view of language the Bible is a very important book. It is the great monument of classical Hebrew; the whole of a nation's early literature, the whole of Hebrew literature, is there. And what is linguistically even more important, the New Testament is the only written example of the colloquial Greek which people spoke to each other every day in the first century. To this we shall return, but, for the moment

briefly, the case is this. When Alexander the Great conquered
the world, he took the Greek language with him; but it obviously
could not be the classical Greek of the great days of Greece. It
was a much simplified form of Greek, called *Koinê* Greek,
which means the Greek of *common* speech. That kind of Greek
did not normally get into literature, and the New Testament is
the only written example of it. In fact, Greek linguists will assert
that, if the New Testament were ever to lose all its religious
value, it would still remain one of the most important linguistic
books in the world.

Once again this is not enough. Even if a book is a linguist's
paradise, that is no guarantee that it will open the way to a far
higher paradise.

4. The Bible is indispensable as a treasury of ethical wisdom.
In the ancient world there was a kind of literature called
Wisdom Literature. The wisdom in question is practical
wisdom; it is the wisdom which enables a man to live honestly
and successfully. The great example of it is the book of
Proverbs; open it anywhere and you will find good advice for
life, and advice written in the most vivid and memorable way.

> My son, do not despise the Lord's discipline
>   or be weary of his reproof.
> The Lord reproves him whom he loves,
>   as a father the son in whom he delights.
> Happy is the man who finds wisdom,
>   and the man who gets understanding,
> for the gain from it is better than the gain from silver,
>   and its profit better than gold.
> She is more precious than jewels,
>   and nothing you desire can compare with her.
> Long life is in her right hand;
>   in her left hand are riches and honour.
> Her ways are ways of pleasantness,
>   and all her paths are peace. (Proverbs 3:11-17)

> Go to the ant. O sluggard;
>   consider her ways and be wise.
> Without having any chief,
>   officer or ruler,
> she prepares her food in summer,
>   and gathers her sustenance in harvest.
> How long will you lie there, O sluggard? .
>   When will you arise from your sleep?
> A little sleep, a little slumber,

A little folding of the hands to rest,
And poverty will come upon you like a vagabond,
  and want like an armed man. (Proverbs 6:6-11)

With proverbs as a guide for practical living, no one need go wrong.

As for the New Testament, always Paul finishes his letters with the most practical of practical advice, and even the non-Christian will often say that we could build heaven on earth, if only people would accept and live the teaching of the Sermon on the Mount.

There is no doubt at all that as a guide to the good life the Bible is supreme; and as a mine of good advice it is inexhaustible. But it is also true that the unfortunate lesson of life is that good advice by itself never made anyone good. If it did, we would have arrived at perfection long ago. To find the unique character of the Bible we must go deeper than the claim that the Bible is an unsurpassable source-book for the conditions of the good life.

5. We come nearer to the heart of the matter, when we make the claim that the Bible is a uniquely effective book. In his book *The Bible in Modern Evangelism* A. M. Chirgwin has a chapter entitled "Achievements" from which the following incidents are selected from among many others.

In Brazil there lived a man called Signor Antonio of Minas. For some time a friend had been pressing him to buy a Bible. He bought one, and thereupon vowed to take it home and burn it. When he reached home he found the fire out, but, he was so eager to burn the book that he rekindled it. Before he threw the book on to the fire, he naturally opened it, so that it would burn the more easily. It opened at the Sermon on the Mount. He paused for a moment to do no more than glance at it. "The words had in them something that held him. He read on, forgetful of time, through the hours of the night, and just as the dawn was breaking he stood up and declared, 'I believe.' "

A New York gangster had been very recently released from prison. He was on his way to join his old gang with a view to another burglary when he stopped to pick a man's pocket in Fifth Avenue. He slipped into Central Park to see what he had acquired. He found himself in possession of a New Testament—no doubt to his deep disappointment. He had time before his appointment, so idly he began to read it, and soon he was deep in the book. A few hours later he went to meet his comrades. He told them what he had been reading, and then once and for all he broke with them and with crime.

Once in a Sicilian forest, in the middle of the night, a colporteur was stopped by a brigand at the point of the revolver. He was ordered by the brigand to light a fire and to burn the books he was carrying. He lit the fire and asked if he might read a little from the books before he burned them. From the first he read the 23rd Psalm; from another the story of the Good Samaritan; from another the Sermon on the Mount; from another the hymn of love. In each case the brigand intervened. "That's a good book," he said. "We won't burn that one. Give it to me." In the end not a book was burned and the brigand went off with the lot. Years later the brigand and the colporteur met again. This time the one-time brigand was an ordained minister of the Christian church. "It was your books that did it," he said to the colporteur.

This is only a brief selection of stories of what the Bible has done. Here, then, there is a book of power, a book operative, effective, dynamic. Here we are coming much nearer to the secret. If a book can do things like that, then it may justly be called unique.

6. We now come to the point of the whole matter, the reason why the ancient book is still relevant and still powerful. The Bible is about the one thing which does not change. Laws and customs change. To some extent even morality changes. For example, the very early parts of the Old Testament have no objection to polygamy, in patriarchal times. To some extent even religion changes. For example, the Jewish religion was a religion of sacrifice, but animal sacrifice is no longer a part of religion for us. The one thing that does not change is personal relationships. So long as people are people, personal relationships will remain the same. Love and hate, loyalty and treachery, fellowship and enmity remain.

This is what the Bible is about. It is about the personal relationship between man and man, between man and woman, and above all between man and God, and God and man; here is why the Bible is ancient and modern at the same time. Take a simple and a lovely example. Jacob had to serve seven years before Laban would give him his daughter to marry. "So Jacob served seven years for Rachel; and they seemed to him but a few days because of the love he had for her" (Genesis 29:20). That is the kind of story, and that is the kind of situation, which will never go out of date, so long as men are men and women are women.

So then the Bible remains forever new because its whole concentration is essentially not upon laws and rules and regulations, but upon men and women and their relationship with each other and their relationship with God. The Bible is the book of love for each other, and love for God—and this is timeless and forever.

7. So this brings us to the last and the supreme reason why the Bible is unique and forever indispensable—a reason to which we shall have cause to return again and again. The Bible is the one place where we find Jesus Christ. The Bible is literally the only source-book for the life and the words and the teaching of Jesus. Take the Bible away, and we would be left with fugitive memories and subjective opinions.

And this is inextricably linked with the last point we made. It is only in and through Jesus Christ that our relationship with our fellowmen is the relationship of love, and that our relationship with God is possible at all.

Ancient in years the Bible is, but it is always relevant, because it deals with the unchanging personal relationships between man and man, man and woman, and man and God, and it is always essential, for in it alone we are confronted with the portrait of the one person in heaven and earth in whom these relationships become what they ought to be.

8. There remains one other thing to be said—and it is said in the Westminster Confession, from which we began. The Confession lays it down that the Bible contains all that is necessary for salvation, and then it goes on to say: "Yet notwithstanding, our full persuasion and assurance of the infallible truth and divine authority thereof, is from the inward work of the Holy Spirit, bearing witness by and with the word in our hearts." And then it goes on to say: "We acknowledge the inward illumination of the Spirit of God to be necessary for the saving understanding of such things as are revealed in the word."

The Jewish doctrine of the Spirit was very simple and very comprehensive. As the Jews saw it, the Spirit did two things. The Spirit revealed God's truth to men, and the Spirit enabled men to recognize that truth, when the truth was revealed. So then, men need the Spirit in their hearts, if they are fully to understand and to appropriate the meaning of the word of God. And that is simply to say that reading and prayer must go hand in hand. We do well to approach the Bible with George Adam Smith's great prayer on our lips:

> Almighty and most merciful God, who hast given the Bible to be the revelation of thy great love to man, and of thy power and will to save him; grant that our study of it may not be made vain by any callousness or carelessness of our hearts, but that by it we may be confirmed in penitence, lifted to hope, made strong for service, and filled with the true knowledge of thee and of thy Son Jesus Christ: this we ask for thy love's sake. Amen.

Chapter 2
The Making of the Old Testament

We are going to begin by studying how the Bible was built up and came into being. To put it in technical language, we are going to study the formation of the *canon* of Scripture. The canon of Scripture is that list of books which have been accepted as the Christian Church's written rule of faith; it is the list of the "official" books of the church; it is the list of books which the church regards as authoritative and determinative for the story of its own history, and for the formation of its life and doctrine.

The word *canon* is itself an interesting word. It comes from a semitic word *kaneh* which means a reed. A straight reed can be used as a rule to draw straight lines. Then the word *canon* goes on to mean a rule, not in the sense of a rule for drawing straight lines, but a rule in the sense of a rule for living a straight life. A canon becomes a rule which decides what is right in any sphere.

But the word *canon* develops another meaning, probably from the fact that the rule which draws straight lines is often marked off in graduations of length. The word *canon* comes to mean a list. For instance, the canon of the Mass is the list of people commemorated in the Mass.

So the canon of Scripture comes to mean the list of the church's authoritative books. But a list in this sense and usage contains books *which have had something done to them;* they have been put on the list; but these same books *do something to everything else;* they become the standard by which all other things are judged. So the canon of Scripture was formulated by the church; in this sense it was not the Bible which made the church, it was the church which made the Bible; for the church existed long before the Bible existed. The early church did not possess the New Testament; it was busy writing it. On the other hand these books are not merely books which have had the passive experience of having had something done to them; they are books which have the active power of guiding and directing the life and work of the church.

So we go on to study how there came into being that list of books which the church accepted as authoritative and which became the basic documents of the Christian faith.

If we go into a shop nowadays and ask for a copy of the Bible, we will be handed one single volume, one book. But if we open that book we will find lists of the books of the Old Testament and of the New Testament. We will find that by the usual reckoning there are thirty-nine books in the Old Testament and twenty-seven in the New Testament, a total of sixty-six books. This is to say that, when we buy a one-volume Bible, we are really buying a library between two covers. When we go on to investigate this portable library a little more closely, we will find that the writing of it was spread over at least one thousand years, and that its books were written all over the ancient world from distant Babylon to Rome.

If we had lived in biblical times, we would never have made the mistake of thinking of the Bible as one book, because we would never have seen it in the form of one book; it did not exist in that form. In the ancient world literary works were written on rolls. The book form, called the *codex,* did not emerge until round about the second century A.D. The Old Testament books were written on skins. The New Testament books were originally written on papyrus. Papyrus was made from the papyrus reed, which grew almost exclusively on the banks of the Nile. It is a bulrush. It can be taller than a man, and thicker than a man's wrist. The pith was cut into long strips; it was then laid down vertically and another row of strips horizontally. It was then moistened; pressure was applied; and there emerged a substance rather like brown-paper, after the papyrus had been smoothed off with pumice stone. *Biblos* or *bublos* is the Greek word from which our word *bible* comes. *Biblos* originally was the word for the papyrus bulrush itself; it then became the word for the papyrus writing material made from that bulrush; it then went on to mean a roll of papyrus; and finally it came to mean a book. Papyrus lasts almost forever, so long as it is kept dry, but it becomes increasingly brittle.

Papyrus was not a cheap material. It was made in sheets which measured about ten by eight inches. It cost anything from five cents a sheet for the cheapest quality to about twenty cents for the best quality, and these prices have to be evaluated in light of the fact that a working-man's wage was eight cents a day. The sheets were joined edge to edge to form a long strip of papyrus. A wooden roller was placed at each end. The roll was unrolled with the one hand, and rolled up again with the other as it was read. The writing was in narrow columns, two and a half to three inches wide.

There is an overlap period when the roll was vanishing and when the book or codex form was coming into use, during which the codex too was made of papyrus. But usually the codex is made of vellum or parchment. Vellum was originally made of calves' skin. *Vitulina charta* it was called, and from that phrase the word *vellum* is derived. Its greatest center of manufacture was Pergamum, and it was also called *Pergamênê charta* from which the word *parchment* is derived.

Parchment and papyrus have one advantage—they are both extremely durable. But the whole situation in the ancient world had two disadvantages.

1. The roll was unwieldy to use. The result is that the maximum length of roll for all practical purposes was thirty feet, and it would take a roll of almost exactly that size to hold the Gospel of Luke or of Matthew, or the book of Acts. This is why no one in the ancient world would ever think of the Old Testament or the New Testament as one book. To such a person the Old and New Testaments would be quite extensive collections of rolls. Even when the codex came in, ancient binding was such that three or four volumes would be needed for even the New Testament. The fact that the Bible is a library would not be lost sight of in the ancient world.

The other disadvantage was expense, both of the papyrus material itself and of the cost of copying.

The unit of measurement for copying was the *stichos* (plural, *stichoi*). A *stichos* was not a line; to pay by the line would not be satisfactory, for different writers might well get a very different number of words into a line. A *stichos* was the average length of one of Homer's hexameter lines which is sixteen syllables. Books were reckoned in *stichoi.* There is a sixth century New Testament manuscript, Codex Claromontanus, which gives the number of *stichoi* in each book. For example, there are 2,900 *stichoi* in Luke, 2,600 in Matthew, 1,040 in Romans, 251 in Colossians, 20 in 2 John, 2,600 in Acts, 1,200 in the Revelation. In the time of Diocletian a price-fixing edict was issued, and the cost of copying was twenty to twenty-five *denarii* per hundred *stichoi.* A *denarius* was about ten cents, so this means it cost about two dollars to copy one hundred lines, which means that Matthew itself, apart from the papyrus, would cost about $50. This costliness was something which remained until printing arrived. There were few who could own a Bible; and until the printed book emerged the Bible could not exist in one volume.

Let us now move on to see the process by which the divine library of the Old Testament came into being and grew up into completeness.

The Jews divided their sacred writings into three sections—the Law, the Prophets, and the Writings. This classification goes back to about 180 B.C. Jesus the son of Sirach had written a book of wisdom which we now commonly call *Ecclesiasticus*. It was originally written in Hebrew. In the year 132 B.C. his grandson, thinking it a valuable book and a book deserving to be widely known, while he was staying in Egypt, translated it into Greek, and in the prologue he refers to the teachings of the Law, the Prophets, and the others who followed them. He speaks again of the Law, the Prophets, and "the other books of our fathers."

The Law consists of the first five books of the Old Testament—Genesis, Exodus, Leviticus, Numbers, Deuteronomy. This section of the Bible is commonly known as the *Pentateuch,* which is a Greek word, meaning the five rolls.

The Prophets came to be divided into two sections. First, there are the Former Prophets. These are the books of Joshua, Judges, Samuel, and Kings. These were reckoned as four books, 1 and 2 Samuel and 1 and 2 Kings, each being reckoned as one book. We usually look on these books as historical books, but the Jews looked on them as prophetic, partly because they tell the story of the great prophets like Elijah and Elisha, and partly because the Jews thought of God as revealing himself in the events of history just as much as, and even more than, in the words of men. Second, there were the Latter Prophets. These were Isaiah, Jeremiah, Ezekiel, and the Twelve. We call the Twelve the Minor Prophets—Hosea, Joel, Amos, Obadiah, Jonah, Micah, Nahum, Habakkuk, Zephaniah, Haggai, Zechariah, Malachi. They are not *minor* in the sense that they are in any way lesser or inferior; they are *minor* only in the sense that they are *shorter* than the first three. The Latter Prophets are also reckoned as four books, because the Twelve are reckoned as one.

The Writings are a miscellaneous collection. They are variously classified. One classification is, first, three books of poetry—Psalms, Proverbs, Job; second, the five *megilloth* (*megillah* means a roll); each of them was connected specially with some great Jewish festival. The Song of Solomon, allegorized to make it speak of the deliverance from Egypt, was associated with the Passover, and was read on the eighth day of the Passover celebrations. Ruth was connected with Pentecost, because it was a harvest idyll, and Pentecost was harvest feast; it was read on the second day of Pentecost. Lamentations was read on 9th Ab, which is the anniversary day of the destruction of Solomon's Temple. Ecclesiastes was read on the third day of the Feast of Tabernacles. Tabernacles commemorated the journey through the wilderness, and during it for a week the people left their houses and lived out of doors in booths made of branches. Ecclesiastes was read to remind men to remember God in the midst of material blessings. Esther was read at the Feast of Purim, for which it provides the reason and the warrant. The five *megilloth* were the only books of the Writings to be read in the synagogue, and they were read only on the occasions with which they were specially connected. Third, there was one book of prophecy—Daniel. Finally, there were two books of history—Ezra-Nehemiah, counting as one, and Chronicles.

The Jews often counted these books as twenty-four. This number was arrived at by reckoning

five books of the Law;

four books of the Former Prophets, 1 and 2 Samuel and 1 and 2 Kings each being reckoned as one book;

four books of the Latter Prophets, the Twelve being reckoned as one book;

eleven books of the Writings, Ezra and Nehemiah, and 1 and 2 Chronicles each being reckoned as one book.

So then let us see how and when each of these three parts of the Old Testament acquired the character of Scripture.

For the Jew the Law was, and is, the most important thing in the world, the center of the Synagogue service, and the essence of all true religion. The word *law* is not quite an adequate title for it; the word *law* is in English too legalistic to describe the Jewish Law. There is much more in it and to it than rules and regulations, prohibitions and commands. The Hebrew word is *Torah,* and it means instruction rather than law. The Torah is God's instruction to men, by obeying which men find life in this world and life in the world to come. They held that the Law had been created before the creation of the world itself, and that God had looked into the Law and then created the world. When the kingdom of God fully came, the Prophets and the Writings would pass away, but the Law would last forever.

It was held to have been delivered to Moses verbatim and entire by the very hand of God himself. It was even held that God began each day by himself setting time apart to study the Law. The aim was that Jewish children should have the Law "graven on their souls." From their infancy they were instructed in the Law, and many a Jew died rather than be false to the Law which to him was nothing less than the word of God. The center of everything was the Law, and even the rest of Scripture, great as it was, was no more than commentary on the Law. The center of the Synagogue service was the reading of the Law. It was read one verse at a time in Hebrew, and translated into whatever language the congregation understood. How then did it reach its exalted position? In what follows we try to reconstruct the situation. This is a reconstruction and not a certainty; but it does fit the facts, and the majority of Old Testament scholars would agree with it.

In regard to the Law we have one date from which we can start, and a dramatic start it is. Religion in Judah had been in a sorry state. The good king Hezekiah had been followed by Manasseh and Amon, who were little better than heathen (2 Kings 21). Their combined reigns lasted for more than half a century, and religion was at its lowest ebb. Then in 621 B.C. the young Josiah came to the throne. And Josiah "did that which was right in the eyes of the Lord." One of the things he did was to initiate the repair and the restoration of the neglected temple; and during that work the book of the Law was found by Hilkiah in the house of the Lord. The reading of that book of the Law moved the king and the people to repentance and reformation, and that book of the Law became for them the very word of God (2 Kings 22 and 23). There is little doubt what that book was. It was the book of Deuteronomy. Someone who was at once prophet and priest wrote it in the dark days of Manasseh and Amon, when it was impossible to speak openly, and then hid it in the temple, to be found in due time.

Here is the beginning of the whole movement; here is the first time that a book is, so to speak, canonized, and becomes the word of God to God's people. There were other statements of the Law, and they too were recovered and collected and cherished. There was the oldest statement of all about the Law, commonly called the little book of the covenant, in Exodus 34.

There was the book of the covenant itself, the conditions to which the people of God agreed, when God took them as his people and promised to be their God. This is found in Exodus 20:22–23:33, and in its present form dates back to 900 B.C. Then in the middle of the sixth century B.C. another great section was added. The very essence of Judaism is in the phrase: "You shall be holy, for I the Lord your God am holy" (Leviticus 19:2). So there arose what is called the Holiness Code. The word *holy* here really means *different*. God is the supremely different one, as he has been called, The Wholly Other. His people too are to be different; they are not to live like other nations; they are to accept the fact that they are a people destined to be different. And the life of difference they are to lead is summed up in the Holiness Code in Leviticus 17 to 26. So we have the great sections of the Law, the voice of God coming ever more fully and directly to his people—the ancient little book of the covenant, and book of the covenant itself, the book of Deuteronomy, and the Code of Holiness. Slowly the Law is building up. It is of the greatest importance to remember one fact that is emerging. People did not sit down and write a book with the intention of writing a book of Scripture. The books which became Scripture had for years and centuries been the help and the strength of the people. These books had already proved themselves over the centuries to be nothing less than the word of God. They were books which by their own proved value had established their right to be recognized as God's word to men. These books which became Scripture were not new books; they were books which time had already proved.

But there is more in the Pentateuch than laws and instruction. The law material in the Pentateuch stands in the context of a narrative which takes the story from the creation of the world to the entry into the Promised Land, and within this narrative there are certain very interesting phenomena. When we study this material, it becomes clear that it is composite and that it comes from more than one source.

Traditionally, it is the work of Moses, but it soon becomes clear that more than Moses had a hand in it. In Genesis there is a list of the kings of Edom, and then there is the sentence, "These are the kings who reigned in the land of Edom, before any king reigned over the Israelites" (Genesis 36:31). The first of the kings is Saul, and Saul is centuries after Moses, so Moses could hardly have spoken of kings reigning over the Israelites.

Genesis 14:14 tells of Abraham's pursuit of his enemies *as far as Dan*. But Dan did not get its name until the time of the Judges (Judges 18:29) after the time of Moses. In Genesis (21:34; 26:14-18) the Philistines are mentioned, but in fact the Philistines did not appear on the scene of history until about 1200 B.C., again after the time of Moses. And, above all in this connection, Deuteronomy 34:1-8 tells of the death of Moses, and it is hardly likely that Moses told the story of his own death!

Unquestionably, Moses was the great law-giver of Israel, but equally unquestionably more than his hand is to be seen in the first five books of the Old Testament. There is more than one narrative here, and there is more than one author here.

There are other signs that the narrative is composite. Often there are two accounts of the same event. There are two stories about how Beer-sheba got its name, one connected with Abraham and one connected with Isaac (Genesis 21:31; 26:31). There are two stories of how Bethel got its name, one telling how Jacob gave it its name on the way to Paddan-aram, the other telling how he gave it its name on the way back from Paddan-aram (Genesis 28:19; 35:15). There are two accounts of the banishment of Hagar and Ishmael, in one of which Hagar is banished *before* the child is born (Genesis 16:6-16), and in the other of which she is banished *after* the child is born (Genesis 21:9-21).

There are two versions of the Creation story. In the one, man is created at the end of the whole process of creation, after the sea and the land and the growing things and the beasts and the birds have been created, and in this version man and woman are created at the same time (Genesis 1). In the other man is created at the beginning of the process; then the garden is created; then the beasts and the birds are formed; then woman is made out of the rib taken from man (Genesis 2). Two stories of the ark in the days of the Flood are interwoven. In the one story the animals are to go into the ark seven pairs of each; in the other story they are to go in in single pairs (Genesis 7:2, 3; 7:8, 9). All over the narrative it can be seen that two versions, two sources, two accounts are being put together. The compiler of the final form is so honest, so full of respect for his sources, that when he has two sources he gives both of them.

Now in this compilation there are times when something else is seen. In Hebrew there are two words for God. There is the word *elôhim*, and there is the word *Jahweh* or *Yahweh*. This latter is very interesting and very important; it is the same word as the word *Jehovah,* which is its much commoner form. In Hebrew there are no vowels in the original script, only consonants, and it was only later that little signs for the vowels were put below the consonants to show what the right pronunciation was. The name of God is represented by the four consonants YHWH. The Jews would never pronounce these four letters as they really sounded; the name of God was too sacred even to be said. Now there was another word *Adonai* which means Lord; and what the Jews did was to take the vowels of the word *Adonai* and to attach them to the sacred letters YHWH, and from that they got the form Jehovah. Jehovah is really the letters YHWH spelled with the vowels of the word for Lord, but the real form is Jahweh (Yahweh), which was too sacred and too holy to say.

In our English translation of the Old Testament, *elôhim* is translated simply God; but YHWH is translated LORD and is printed in special capital letters, as for instance in Genesis 2:4, 5. This way of printing LORD for Jahweh, or Jehovah, is used in the Authorized Version, the Revised Standard Version, and the New English Bible. Now when we examine these early books carefully we find that in some sections God is called *elôhim,* God, and in some sections he is called Jahweh, LORD. For instance, right at the beginning of the Bible, in the first Creation story God is called *elôhim,* God (Genesis 1:1–2:3), whereas in the second Creation story God is called Jahweh, LORD (Genesis 2:4-24). We saw that in the ark story of the Flood there is one version of the story in which the animals are taken in in seven pairs and another in which the animals are taken in in single pairs. In the version in which the animals are taken in in seven pairs the command is given by the LORD, Jahweh (Genesis 7:1, 2); in the version in which the animals go in in single pairs the command is given by God, *elôhim* (Genesis 7:9). So we find that in the very early parts of the Bible there are two interwoven sources, in one of which God is called *elôhim,* and in the other of which he is called Jahweh; that is to say in one source God is called God, and in the other he is called LORD. After a time both sources call God Jahweh, LORD, for in the source which began by calling God *elôhim,* God, we find the famous story of how Moses discovered that the name of God is Jahweh, the One Who Is (Exodus 3:13-16), for this was the lesson that Moses received in the mysterious incident of the burning bush (Exodus 3:1-6).

What becomes clear is that the Law, the Pentateuch, did not

spring into being ready-made. It is the product of the centuries. It is the essence and the distillation of the voice of God to men both in words and in events over the years. Here is the concentrated voice of God over the centuries—first the little book of the covenant; then the larger book of the covenant; then Deuteronomy; then the Holiness Code; then the story of the ways of God to men compiled by the two different writers; then its molding and interweaving into one, with that complete honesty which would omit nothing and change nothing; until in the end there emerged that wonderful amalgam of law and history which to the Jew was and is the word of God as nothing else on earth.

But there remains one question still to ask. When did the Law stop being simply a wonderful book, and when did it become Scripture? When did it stop being only a book and become a Bible? This is to ask, when did the oldest part of the Bible begin to be regarded as definitely the word of God? There are three indications to help us to fix a date.

1. One of the great dates was the date when the Old Testament was translated into Greek. We shall tell the story of that translation later. At the present moment we are concerned only with the date when the Septuagint, as the Greek translation of the Old Testament is called, came into being. It is obviously a great date. When the Old Testament remained in Hebrew its sphere was strictly limited to the Jews; when it was translated into Greek it became the possession of the world. The Old Testament was translated into Greek in the reign of Ptolemy the Second, called Philadelphus, in Egypt, and this Ptolemy reigned from 285 until 246 B.C. At first, it was only the Law which was translated, for it was the Law above all which was Scripture for the Jew by that time. We can therefore begin by saying that the Law was certainly Scripture by about 270 B.C. Can we trace it further back?

2. The Samaritans even to the present day accept only the Law, the Pentateuch, as Scripture; they do not so accept the rest of the Old Testament. This will mean that they split from the rest of the nation when the Law had become Scripture, but the rest of the Old Testament had not. The Samaritan split dates to about 400 B.C. Therefore away back in 400 B.C. the Law was already regarded as the word of God.

3. When we read Nehemiah 8–10 we find Ezra the scribe

reading "the book of the Law" to the people, and the people taking it as the Law of God and the law of their lives. This happened after they had returned from exile. From then on the Jews were to be forever the people of the Book, and that book, the book of the Law. And that also happened about 400 B.C.

Everything points to the fact that the Law became Scripture, the Law was established as the word of God to men, four hundred years before Jesus came into the world as a man. We may take it that men have regarded the Law, the Pentateuch, the first five books of the Old Testament, as Scripture since 400 B.C. For very nearly 2,400 years men have found the word of God in the books of the Law. And there is something unique about a book by which men have guided their lives not only for hundreds but for thousands of years.

It will be remembered that we began the story of the formation of the Old Testament by seeing that the Jews divided it into three sections—the Law, the Prophets, and the Writings. We have now seen how the Law was built up and how by 400 B.C. it had become Scripture, and now we turn our attention to the Prophets.

As we have seen, to the Jew the Law was incomparably the greatest part of Scripture; for most modern students of the Bible the Prophets would stand higher than the Law. They would indeed, with the exception of the Psalms, be the most precious part of the Old Testament for most of us. Let us see then how they too became part of the word of God.

We have already seen that the Prophets were divided into two sections—the Former Prophets, and the Latter Prophets. The Former Prophets consist of the books of Joshua, Judges, Samuel, and Kings. The authors of these books are completely unknown. There are not even any traditional titles ascribed to them as the books of the Law are all ascribed to Moses. But Jewish tradition did say that Joshua wrote the book of Joshua, that Samuel wrote the book of Judges and Samuel, and that Jeremiah wrote the books of Kings. These four books, as the Jews reckoned them, were completed in the sixth and the fifth centuries B.C.

It may seem strange to us to find what we regard as history books ranked among the prophetic books. There are two reasons for this. These books tell of the great prophets who functioned before the literary prophets emerged, the non-literary prophets—Samuel and Nathan and Elijah and Elisha.

They certainly had prophetic material in them. Second, the Jews took history very seriously. For them the events of history were God in action; history for them was the arena of the activity of God. God, for them, was speaking in events. The events of history were, for them, the demonstration of the truth of the prophetic message. History too was for them the voice of God. History for them was the voice of God proclaiming across the centuries that it is well with the good, and it is disaster for the wicked. It was perfectly natural to look on history as prophetic, for history was for them the manifestation of the rule of God.

When we come to the Latter Prophets, the great named prophets, it is well to have a time scheme in our minds as we read them, and to know the events of history which were the background of their writings.

First of them to come in the latter half of the eighth century, were Amos and Micah. They were writing near the days when the Assyrians invaded Palestine and when the Kingdom of Samaria was wiped out forever in 722 B.C. These two prophets strike the note which is from beginning to end the center of the prophetic message. That message is summed up in a famous phrase—it was the proclamation of *ethical monotheism.* Let us take the second word first, the word *monotheism.* There are three forms of men's belief in God. First, there is *polytheism. Polloi* is the Greek for many; *theos* is the Greek for God or a god; and *polytheism* is the word which describes a religion which has many gods. This was the way of the early Greek and Roman religion with Zeus and Apollo and Athene and Aphrodite and all the rest of them. This is the stage of many gods. Second, there is *henotheism.* At this stage men still believed in many gods, but they had come to believe that only one of these gods was valid for them. Each country had its own god, and beyond that country the writ of that god did not run. So each country had its own god, but no one denied that the gods of the other countries were equally real and in their own sphere equally powerful. So Jephthah says to the Ammonites: "Will you not possess what Chemosh your god gives you to possess? And all that the Lord (Jahweh) our God has dispossessed before us we will possess" (Judges 11:24). At this stage Jahweh was the only God for the Hebrews, but that did not mean that Chemosh was not real enough for the Ammonites. At this stage a nation had its own god, and for them that god was the only god, but there was no denial of the rights of other gods in regard to other nations.

Lastly, there is the belief in *monotheism,* which is the belief that there is only one God, who is the God of all men, the God of this universe and of any other universe that does exist or ever will exist.

This was the first message of the Prophets, the message that there is one God and one God only, and to him Israel must be true. Nor was this altogether easy. In the days when men believed that each country had its own god, then when a man came to stay in a strange country he brought, as it were, his own god with him, and built a shrine for him. This is what happened in the case of Solomon. In the days of Solomon, Israel was politically a great nation. This led to foreign alliances. Very often a foreign alliance was cemented by the king of the one country marrying the daughter of the king of the other. This is exactly what Solomon did, and these foreign princesses brought their own gods and goddesses with them and so infected the true religion with false faiths (1 Kings 11:1-8). To us monotheism is the only natural belief; in the days of the prophets it was a great discovery, and the prophets were the guardians of it.

Not only did these great early prophets teach monotheism; they also taught *ethical* monotheism. Nowadays religion and morality go hand in hand. But strangely in the ancient days religion and immorality were apt to go hand in hand. Take three instances of this. In the ancient world, when a man founded a new city, it was the custom to lay the foundations of it, and to fix the gateposts of it, in the body of his slaughtered and sacrificed son (1 Kings 16:34). In the worship of the god Molech little children were sacrificed in the fire (2 Kings 23:10). The worship of Baal was the worship of the fertility cult. The baals were the powers who made the corn grow, and the grape ripen. The greatest fertility force of all is sex. So to the temples of the baals there were attached many sacred priestesses who were nothing other than sacred prostitutes, and to have sexual intercourse with one of them was an act of worship. These so-called priestesses were the cult-prostitutes whom Hosea condemns (Hosea 4:14). The prophets had to teach men that the most elaborate ritual in the world is no substitute for personal chastity, for social justice, and for love for man and love for God. The whole book of Amos has been called "a cry for social justice," and no text in the Bible is better known than Micah's saying that God does not want sacrifice. What he wants is that men should do justice, and love kindness, and walk humbly with him (Micah 6:6-8). For us these things are part of religion. For the great early prophets they were epoch-making discoveries. The prophets were the great ethical monotheists, insisting that there is one God, and that chastity, mercy, and fidelity are the true sacrifices.

Also from the eighth century B.C. come two more of the great early prophets, and they too have their dominant ideas. As we have seen, the great cry of Amos and Micah is the insistence on social justice. But Hosea is above all the prophet of undefeatable love. Hosea argued from himself to God. Hosea had taken on God's orders a wife from the streets. He treated her with love, but she went back to her old life; but every time she went back, he took her back again, with a love which would not own defeat. And, so Hosea argued, if I a man can love like that, how much more God?

So we have Amos and Micah with their stress on social justice; and we have Hosea with his stress on love. But there is still another of the great eighth-century prophets. The book of Isaiah falls into three parts, and the first part of it (chapters 1–39) belongs to this same period. Isaiah was an aristocrat and the friend of kings, and he too has his dominant note; and his note is holiness. "Holy, holy, holy is the Lord of hosts" (Isaiah 6:3). Always he confronts men with the holy God. And always he too is insistent that nothing can take the place of justice and of love. Sacrifices, new moons, sabbaths, prayers—by themselves they are without avail.

> Seek justice,
>   correct oppression;
> defend the fatherless,
>   plead for the widow. (Isaiah 1:10-17)

So each of the great eighth-century prophets has his note—Amos and Micah, social justice; Hosea, love; Isaiah, holiness; and it is while remembering their note that we should read them.

In the seventh and the sixth centuries B.C. there was another group of prophets, proclaiming the word of God in the light of their contemporary history, and always interpreting that history in the light of the purpose of God. In 627 B.C. Zephaniah saw the Scythian hordes arriving from the East, and saw in that invasion the beginning of the time of judgment for Assyria, and for Moab and for Philistia, and for Judah too. It was for him the warning of the coming of the Day of the Lord. At the same time Nahum was vividly portraying the fall of Nineveh. For a moment it looked as if God was going to strike in history, but the event was the rise of still another great power, the rise of Babylon, and Habakkuk writes wondering at the delay of God, as one tyranny succeeds aother.

Then there came two of the greatest of the prophets who both made the discovery which saved Jewish religion from collapse. Jeremiah saw the fall of Jerusalem at the hands of the Babylonians in 586 B.C., and Ezekiel lived through the exile with the people in Babylon, where he dreamed of the new order of things which would some day be. But the great contribution of these two was the reminder that religion is not only a national thing; it is a personal thing too, and that even more.

It is hard for us to understand, but it took centuries for the individual fully to emerge. For centuries men did not think of themselves principally as individuals; they thought of themselves as members of the group or the tribe or the family or the nation to which they belonged. A very good Old Testament example of that is the story of the sin of Achan. In spite of the command of God to destroy all the spoils of Jericho, Achan kept some. The consequence was disastrous. Disaster fell on the nation. It was discovered that it was Achan who was guilty, and, when that discovery had been made, Achan "and his sons and his daughters and his oxen and asses and sheep, and his tent and all that he had" were utterly destroyed (Joshua 7:1-26). The punishment fell not simply on the man but on the whole group.

A modern example of all this comes from Australia. The Australian aborigines are among the most primitive of people left in the world, and, until quite recently, if you asked an aborigine his name, it was not his name that he would tell you; it was his tribe: "I am a man of such and such a tribe," he would say.

Now, if you think always in terms of the group, then if the nation is in the midst of disaster, faith may well collapse; but, if you make the discovery that a man is connected with God, not because he is the member of a nation or a tribe, but because he is a person, then the connection between the individual and God can survive any national trial or disaster. This is exactly what Jeremiah and Ezekiel discovered. They discovered that a man was connected with God, not because he was a Jew, but because he was a man. They discovered personal religion. Like all great discoveries it is a very simple discovery, but few could be more important.

But a new world power was emerging, the power of Persia, and the second section of Isaiah has something of quite extraordinary interest to say about this; the section is chapters 40 to 55. The leader of the Persians was Cyrus who had no intention of liberating the Jews from the power of Babylon, and it is very unlikely that Cyrus had ever heard of Jahweh, or would have thought Jahweh of any importance, if he had heard of him. But in spite of that Cyrus has his place in the plan and the purpose of God. God says of Cyrus: "He is my shepherd, and he shall fulfil all my purpose." Cyrus is the anointed whose right hand God has grasped (Isaiah 44:28; 45:1). Cyrus was to be the liberator of the Jews. He did not know it, but he was working out the purposes of God. Here indeed is a philosophy of history. All history is in the hand of God, and even the man who has never heard of God may be, all unknown to himself, the servant of God and the instrument in the hand of God. Truly, a man can face the world with a faith like that.

It is in this section of Isaiah that we find the picture of the Suffering Servant, that figure who was to have so great an influence on the thought of the New Testament, and almost certainly on the thought of Jesus himself. The picture of the Suffering Servant culminates in Isaiah 53 in the one who was wounded for our transgressions and bruised for our iniquities (Isaiah 53:5). The complete picture of the Suffering Servant is drawn in what are known as the four Servant Songs (Isaiah 42:1-4; 49:1-6; 50:4-9; 52:13–53:12). It is to be noted that in Isaiah 53 all the verbs up to verse 10 are in the past tense. On the face of it, they are a description of someone whom the prophet knew and who had suffered, rather than of someone who was to come. It is true that sometimes a prophet was so sure that what he was saying was going to happen that he spoke of it as having already happened, but Isaiah 53 does not read like that.

Who was the sufferer in Isaiah 53? This is one of the questions which has always fascinated and eluded the minds of scholars. The best book on the subject is C. R. North's *The Suffering Servant in Deutero-Isaiah,* and in it North tells us that S. R. Driver, the great Old Testament scholar, planned to write a commentary on Isaiah, and abandoned the task because of the

tangled maze of interpretations in regard to the Servant
Is the Servant Isaiah himself, who according to Jewish tradition was martyred and buried in a felon's grave, as the Ethiopian thought it might be (Acts 8:34)? Is he Jeremiah who speaks of himself as "a gentle lamb led to the slaughter" (Jeremiah 11:19)? Is he Jehoiachin who according to Jewish tradition sacrificed himself to Nebuchadnezzar in order to save the city of Jerusalem from devastation (2 Kings 24:8-20)? Is he Zerubbabel who after playing a foremost part in the return from exile strangely vanishes from history (Haggai 1:1, 12, 14; 2:21-23; Zechariah 4:6-10)? Or is the Servant the nation of Israel, redemptively suffering for its own sins and the sins of the world? We cannot tell, but we do know beyond a doubt that this figure of the Suffering Servant found its complete fulfilment in Jesus Christ. All over the New Testament Jesus is identified with the Suffering Servant (Acts 3:13; 3:26; 4:27, 30; 8:26-35; Matthew 8:14-17; 12:14-21; Luke 22:37; 2 Corinthians 5:21; 1 Peter 1:19; 2:22-25). No Old Testament figure is so built into the New Testament as the Suffering Servant of Second Isaiah.

So we have the rise of another world power. Assyria had left the scene and so had Babylon, and now it was the turn of Persia to dominate the stage of history. This was very important for the Jews, for the Persians allowed the Jews to return to Jerusalem, from which the Babylonians had removed them in exile, so in the late sixth century and in the fifth century we find Haggai and Zechariah urging them on to rebuild the shattered temple, and to try to restore the lost glory.

We find Obadiah condemning Edom because she had stood aside and seen Judah reduced to slavery. We find Joel cheering the people when days were difficult, and Malachi rousing them to new devotion, when devotion had grown cold. In the slackening of devotion the people had come to try to put God off with second-bests, and with the cheapest and the shoddiest things they could offer (Malachi 1:6-14). And in the day of despair and depression Malachi tried to rekindle the flame of devotion in their hearts.

There is one book included among the prophets which we have not yet mentioned—the book of Jonah. This little book is one of the greatest books in the Old Testament, because it calls on the Jews to abandon their exclusiveness, to bring God's word to the Gentiles, to rejoice when the Gentiles accept the message, to believe that even Nineveh can be saved, if Nineveh repents.

onah is the one supremely missionary book in the Old Testament. It is also one of the latest books for it comes most probably from the fourth century B.C.

We have now to ask when the books of the prophets ceased to be merely precious works of devotional literature and became Scripture.

1. We have to note regarding the prophets that which we have noted about the other books of the Old Testament. Long before they became Scripture they were known and used and loved. It was because they had proved their power to illuminate the mind and to comfort and strengthen the heart that they did earn a place in Scripture.

It was in the days of the exile that the works of the prophets came to be known and loved. This was so because these books did two things. They foretold the fate of the sinner and of the disobedient and of those who forsook the way of God for their own way. And that part of them had been amply fulfilled. The nation knew only too well now what happened to a nation which disregarded the voice of God. What the prophets had said would happen had happened. But the prophets did not end their message there. Just as they had a message of doom for the disobedient, so they had a message of hope for the penitent. And the Jews had the conviction that just as the message of doom had come true, so the message of hope would also come true. F. C. Grant in his book *How to Read the Bible* (pp. 84, 85) points out that the prophetic message follows a pattern:

(a) Your sins are about to find you out, justice is certain to overtake you—soon; (b) if God's punishment is severe, he is still concerned with those whom he punishes, and his purpose is to save, not to annihilate; (c) in this final hour before the stroke of doom, repent!—for, if you repent, God may turn away the threatened punishment and restore you to his favour; (d) indeed, God, who foresees all things is aware that a "remnant" will survive, a penitent few, like the living stump of a fallen tree; out of this small handful he will be able to build up once more the nation or the family or the covenant-people of his choice.

In other words, the message of the prophets was compounded in equal parts of threat and promise, of doom and rescue, of the midnight and the dawn. And so the Jews read and studied and drew strength from the prophets in the certainty that, if the prophets had been right about the doom, they would also be right about the restoration. In the darkest days they drew their hope from the prophetic hope.

2. But these prophetic books drew their special place from another factor in the situation. They were regarded as the great examples of a voice that was now silenced forever. No longer was there anyone to say: "Thus saith the Lord." As the Psalmist said wistfully: "We do not see our signs; there is no longer any prophet, and there is none among us who knows how long" (Psalm 74:9). By the time of Zechariah it was true that anyone who claimed to be a prophet was to be regarded as a fraud: "And if anyone again appears as a prophet, his father and mother who bore him will say to him, 'You shall not live, for you speak lies in the name of the Lord'; and his father and mother who bore him shall pierce him through when he prophesies" (Zechariah 13:3). So in 1 Maccabees it is said: "Thus there was great distress in Israel, such as had not been since the time that prophets ceased to appear among them" (1 Maccabees 9:27). Simon is made leader and priest, "until a trustworthy prophet should arise" (1 Maccabees 14:41). They will wait until a prophet comes and tells them what to do (1 Maccabees 4:46). There came a time as early as the fourth century B.C. when the prophets belonged to the splendor of the past; they had spoken with a voice and an accent which was forever silent. Obviously this gives them a greatness which could never be repeated.

3. When then did they actually come to be regarded as Scripture? This is something which we can only deduce. In 2 Maccabees 2:13 it is said of Nehemiah that "he also founded a library and collected the books about the kings and prophets, and the writings of David and letters of kings about votive offerings." It was always part of Jewish tradition that Ezra had a great deal to do with the construction of the collection of Scripture. This is no more than tradition, but it may well be that at that time—about 400 B.C.—the writings of the prophets were collected and set in order.

But there is one fact which may well give us our clue. Daniel is clearly a prophetic book; it is a book which characteristically foretells the future. And yet the strange fact is that in Jewish practice Daniel was never ranked with the Prophets but always with the Writings. This can only mean that Daniel comes from a time when the list of the prophets was closed. If that list had been open, surely Daniel would have been on it. Now the date of Daniel is about 165 B.C., and this is an indication that the list of the prophets was probably closed by the time. So it is likely that the prophets came to be regarded as Scripture by round about 200 B.C.

Slowly the Old Testament is being built up; slowly book after book is gaining admittance, because it could not be denied, and because it bore its inspiration on its face. By about 400 B.C. the Law was Scripture; and probably by 200 B.C. the Prophets stood beside the Law. It only remains to see how the Writings won their place.

So then let us turn our attention to these Writings. There were, as we have already noted, eleven of them—Psalms, Proverbs, Job, Ecclesiastes, the Song of Solomon, Ruth, Lamentations, Esther, Ezra-Nehemiah, Chronicles, Daniel. The Writings do not form a unified and homogeneous group like the Law or the Prophets. They are very much a miscellaneous collection, a miscellany, as someone has called them, of independent books. They never quite attained to the place of the other two groups. Some of them had their place on special occasions in the synagogue worship, but they were not read regularly and systematically at the synagogue services as the Law and the Prophets were. When the Jews spoke about their Scriptures, they usually spoke about the Law and the Prophets, but to fulfil them (Matthew 5:17). He said that the principle which commands us to do to others as we would have them do to us is the Law and the Prophets (Matthew 7:12). It was the Law and the Prophets which preceded the coming of the Kingdom (Luke 16:16). It was Moses and all the Prophets which Jesus expounded and interpreted on the way to Emmaus (Luke 24:27). It is the Law and the Prophets which are read in the synagogue (Acts 13:15). If in the New Testament another section is added to Scripture, it is the Law, the Prophets, and the Psalms (Luke 24:44).

In the Writings there was something of everything. E. J. Goodspeed in *How Came the Bible?* (p. 39) divides them into philosophical discussion of religion—Job and Ecclesiastes; dirges—Lamentations; love songs—the Song of Solomon; stories—Ruth and Esther; history written from the priestly point of view—Chronicles. F. C. Grant in *How to Read the Bible* (p. 87) distinguishes poetry—Job, Psalms, Song of Solomon, Lamentations; Wisdom books—Ecclesiastes and Proverbs; stories—Esther and Ruth; a prophetic book—Daniel; history—Ezra-Nehemiah and Chronicles. In the Writings we really have the religious literature of a nation, and they won their place, not as a single whole, but piece-meal.

We have first to ask how they got into Scripture at all. We saw that from the fourth century onward it was the conviction of the Jews that the direct voice of God had ceased to speak. Now this would in effect mean that no book written after Ezra had any chance of becoming Scripture. It lay outside the period of direct inspiration. The rabbis arrived at an odd conclusion about this. If the author of a book was known, and if he was known to have written outside the period of inspiration, then the book did not get into the list of books which were Scripture. That is what kept out Ecclesiasticus, which is one of the very great books, and the omission of which many regret. It was known to be the writing of one Jesus the son of Sirach, and that he wrote it about 180 B.C. and that his grandson translated it into Greek about 132 B.C. Its date and author were known, and therefore it was out. On the other hand, the rabbis held that if the author of a book was unknown, and if it was a book of sufficient religious value to make it desirable as Scripture, then it was possible to attribute it to one of the great figures who did fall within the period of inspiration. Thus since no one really knew who wrote them, Ruth could be attributed to Samuel; Lamentations to Jeremiah; Proverbs and Ecclesiastes to Solomon; Job to Moses; the Song of Solomon to Solomon, or at least to the time of Hezekiah; all the Psalms to David, although in the middle of the book we find the verse, "The prayers of David, the son of Jesse, are ended" (Psalm 72:20); Ezra and Nehemiah to Ezra. The place that Ezra acquired in Jewish tradition was unique. The rabbis said: "The Torah was forgotten by Israel, until Ezra went up from Babylon and re-established it," and they also held that, if the Law had not already been given to Moses, Ezra was fit to have received it. To Ezra's place in tradition we will return. It is indeed fortunate that the Jewish rabbis found a way to preserve these books, for otherwise they might well have vanished.

We shall now look at the process by which these Writings were established as Scripture, and then after that we shall look at them individually. There are five pieces of evidence which will combine to give us our date.

1. We have already had cause to cite what 2 Maccabees 2:13 says about Nehemiah. It says of him that he founded a library and collected the books about the kings and the prophets and the writings of David. If this is to be taken as historical, then we

could say that Nehemiah began the collection of the Psalms, and thereby laid the foundation of that section of Scripture which became the Writings.

2. We have also referred before to the prologue which the grandson of Jesus son of Sirach wrote to his Greek translation of his grandfather's book. In that prologue he refers to the great things handed down—the writings of the Law and the prophets and of others who have followed in their steps. He tells how his grandfather had studied the Law and the Prophets and the books of our fathers. He speaks of the Law and the Prophets and the rest of the books. He never uses the term the Writings, but it is clear that for him there was in addition to the Law and the Prophets a third section of Scripture.

3. As we have already noted in Luke 24:44 Jesus is said to have expounded to his disciples after his resurrection the things about himself in the Law of Moses, the Prophets, and the Psalms.

4. In the apocryphal book 4 Ezra, called in the printed Apocrypha 2 Esdras, there is a highly colored fictional account of the work of Ezra (chapter 14). In Ezra's time the Law had been lost, and it was Ezra's divinely appointed task to restore it. He was taken to a field with five men and given a cup of liquid like fire to drink. For forty days and forty nights he dictated non-stop to the five men. During that time ninety-four books were written. Then the Most High said to him: "Make public the twenty-four books that you wrote first and let the worthy and the unworthy read them; but keep the seventy that were written last, in order to give them to the wise among your people." This is obvious legend, but the point is that when this book of 4 Ezra was written in the latter half of the first century A.D. the Jewish Scriptures were composed of twenty-four books, which is the number including the Writings. By that time the Writings were Scripture.

5. Round about A.D. 100 Josephus the Jewish historian laid it down that the Jewish books were fixed and settled, with none to be added and none to be subtracted.

This all fits in, for it is usually held that it was in A.D. 90 at the Council of Jamnia, near Jaffa, that the Jewish rabbis finally fixed the contents of Scripture. The Writings were now complete.

When we remember how varied a miscellany the Writings

are, we will not be surprised to learn that they did not all become Scripture with the same speed and the same unanimity.

About some of them there never was any question. There was never any question about the Psalms. The Psalms were the hymnbook and the prayer book of the temple. They were intimately connected with the worship and the liturgy of the temple. Each day of the week had its special psalm with a rabbinic reason to explain its attachment.

Psalm 24 was the psalm for the first day of the week. "The earth is the Lord's and the fullness thereof"—this commemorated the first day of creation, "when God possessed the world and ruled in it." Psalm 48 was the psalm for the second day of the week. "Great is the Lord and greatly to be praised"—because on the second day of creation "God divided his works and reigned over them." Psalm 82 was the psalm for the third day of the week. "God has taken his place in the divine council"—"because on that day the earth appeared on which are the Judge and the judged." Psalm 94 was the psalm for the fourth day. "O Lord, thou God of vengeance"—"because on the fourth day God made the sun, moon and stars, and will be avenged on those that worship them." Psalm 81 was the psalm for the fifth day. "Sing aloud to God our strength"—"because of the variety of creatures created on that day to praise his name." Psalm 93 was the psalm for the sixth day. "The Lord reigns"—"because on that day God finished his works and made man, and the Lord ruled over all his works." For the seventh day, the sabbath, the psalm was Psalm 92. "It is good to give thanks to the Lord"—"because the sabbath is symbolic of the day, when after the six thousand years dispensation, God will reign over all, and his glory and service will fill the earth with thanksgiving."

Both for public worship and for private devotion the Psalms stood supreme, and never was their right to a place within Scripture challenged.

The five rolls, the *Megilloth,* which were connected with the great festivals and memorials had a secure place, although as we shall see some of them were challenged.

Chronicles, Job, Ezra-Nehemiah, and Daniel had a special place, because the high priest read publicly from them on the eve of the greatest of all Jewish religious occasions, the Day of Atonement.

Three books were particularly questioned. The Song of

Solomon came under question, because, unless it is read as an allegory, which it was originally never meant to be, it is a passionate love poem of very physical love, indeed one of the supreme love poems of the world. Ecclesiastes came under question because of its weary pessimism. Do your best here, and live your hardest here, is its message, because there is nothing on the other side of death but the land of shadows (Ecclesiastes 9:10). Esther came under question, because, extraordinary as it may seem, the name of God is never mentioned in it from beginning to end, and it is the warrant for the Festival of Purim, which commemorates the victory of Mordecai over Haman, but which is not one of the festivals laid down in the Law at all.

But after the Council of Jamnia the doubts were stilled and the questions were silenced.

So then, in the guidance and the providence of God the Old Testament reached its present form. And we may well note three things about it.

1. It is composed of books, which before they entered the sacred realm of Scripture, had stood the test of the years. It was not that a man wrote a book with the intention of writing a book which should be Scripture. The man wrote his book; he delivered it to men and to the years. Throughout the years and the centuries men came to love that book and to stay their hearts on it, and God used that book for his purposes. And then there came a day when men recognized that that book was nothing less than a message of God. If we liked to do so, we could say that books became Scripture by the principle of the survival of the fittest. A book became part of the Bible because it was so effective and so obviously used by God that none could stop it.

2. We must always remember that it took from the eighth century to the second century to write the Old Testament. Think of that in terms of modern history. The equivalent would be a book which men began to write in the fourteenth century and finished writing in the twentieth century. This is something to which we must return, but it is easy to see the difference in the world between 1300 and 1900. Six hundred years is a long time.

3. Further, the establishment of the Old Testament as Scripture began with the finding of Deuteronomy in 621 B.C. and ended with the Council of Jamnia in A.D. 90. This is to say that it took rather more than seven hundred years to build up the Old Testament to the point when there was a canon of Scripture. The roots of the Old Testament go very deep.

42

Chapter 3
The Making of the New Testament

The New Testament as we now possess it consists of twenty-seven books. There are four Gospels, one book of church history, twenty-one letters, and one apocalypse. The first time we meet the New Testament exactly in this shape is in A.D. 367. The great bishop Athanasius was accustomed at Easter time to send a pastoral letter to his people. In the year 367 he decided to deal with the books which it was right and proper for a Christian to read and which the church approved. He listed them, and for the first time the list contains all the books which make up our New Testament. This is to say that the making of the New Testament took more than three hundred years to complete.

From the beginning of its existence, the Christian faith was the faith of a book. Christianity was cradled in Judaism, and Judaism was centered in the synagogue. In its very earliest days the Christian church had no intention of breaking away from the ancestral worship of the Jews. We find Peter and John on their way up to pray in the temple (Acts 3:1). We find that both Stephen and Paul began their career as preachers by debating in the synagogue (Acts 6:8-10; 9:20, 21). The center of the synagogue service was the reading of the Scripture. That is what the service existed for. It began with a recital of the creed of Judaism and with the offering of a series of prayers. It ended with an address by a Rabbi or a distinguished stranger. But right in the middle there came the reading of Scripture, and it was for this that the people had assembled.

When it was no longer possible for the Christians to worship in the synagogue, when the doors of the synagogue were closed against them, they took the form of the synagogue service with them. More than that—they took the book of the synagogue service with them too. In the early days of the church the New Testament had not yet been written. It was not the New Testament which produced the church; it was the church which produced the New Testament. So, in the beginning, it was the Old Testament which was read every Sunday at the Christian services, and usually it was read in the form of its Greek translation, the Septuagint, which is usually denoted by the letters LXX. So in the first days of the church it was the Old Testament which was the book of the church; it was the Old Testament which was quoted and read.

For example in Peter's sermon at Pentecost (Acts 2:14-40) ten out of twenty-seven verses are Old Testament quotations—Acts 2:17-21 = Joel 2:28-32; Acts 2:25-28 = Psalm 16:8-11; Acts 2:34, 35 = Psalm 110:1. In Paul's sermon in Antioch (Acts 13:16-41) nine out of twenty-six verses go back to the Old Testament—Acts 13:16-22 is a straight summary out of Old Testament history up to David; Acts 13:33 = Psalm 2:7; Acts 13:34 = Isaiah 55:3; Acts 13:35 = Psalm 16:10; Acts 13:41 = Habakkuk 1:5; Acts 13:47 = Isaiah 49:6. In the early days it was the Old Testament which was the sacred book of the Church.

How then did the New Testament arise at all? First of all, let us see in what order the New Testament was written. The most interesting fact to begin with is that the letters of Paul were almost certainly written before any of the rest of the New Testament. They were written between the years—approximately—A.D. 49 and A.D. 62.

Paul's letters were real letters. For the most part they were written to meet a local and a temporary situation. Something went wrong in Thessalonica or in Corinth, and Paul wrote to correct the situation. F. C. Grant has said truly; "Had telephones been invented, Paul certainly would have used them—and we should never have had any epistles from his pen!" (*How to Read the Bible,* p. 131). Paul wrote to correct some situation in Thessalonica or Galatia or Corinth. He wrote as a pastor, not as an author. And it must be remembered that Paul was writing long before the days of printing. His letters *were* letters, handwritten because there was no such thing as print, existing to begin with as one single copy, often written to correct some temporary, local situation in which things had gone wrong. Of course, Paul dealt with the local and temporary situation in the light of eternal truth, but nonetheless his letters were letters in the real sense of the term, and there is nothing so temporary and local and evanescent as a letter. It is always of the first importance to remember that there was no question of Paul *publishing* his letters in a modern sense.

How then did they ever become Scripture? What follows is necessarily a reconstruction. It is not certainty, but it does seem to meet the facts. We begin by remembering that for the mos part Paul's letters existed in the churches to which they were sent and nowhere else. They were not published as books; they were sent as letters. How were they ever rescued and recovered and published? It was probably about A.D. 90 when the book of Acts was published. Now it is a strange thing that if we had no more than the book of Acts we would never have known that Paul ever wrote a letter. Acts has absolutely nothing to say about Paul as a letter-writer. What likely happened was that, when Acts was published, it was suddenly realized what an extraordinary figure Paul was. Suddenly Paul came to life, and in consequence of that every church which had a letter of Paul suddenly realized over again what a treasure it had; and so the letters were searched for and collected and shared and became the possession of the church at large rather than merely the correspondence of a congregation. We may well take it that it was the publication of Acts which showed the greatness of Paul, and which was the mainspring of the movement to collect his letters. At this stage, about A.D. 90, Paul's letters have not yet been ranked as Scripture, but they have become one of the most treasured possessions of the church.

So then Paul's letters were written between A.D. 49 and A.D. 62, and they were probably rediscovered in all their greatness as a consequence of the publication of Acts about A.D. 90. But what was happening to the rest of the New Testament, and in particular what was happening to the Gospels? Roughly speaking, the dates of the Gospels in the form in which we have them are A.D. 65–70 for Mark; A.D. 80–90 for Matthew and Luke; A.D. 100 for John. Why were they so long in being written, and why were they so long in becoming the books of the church? And what in the end did cause them finally to be written?

1. In the first place, Christianity was born into a nonliterary civilization, at least in its early stages. It came into the world long before the invention of printing, and there was no way of really mass-producing books as can be done in modern times. People did not think in terms of the mass production of books as they do nowadays. This was specially true of Judaism. The rabbis had the strongest possible objection to writing down their teaching. "Commit nothing to writing," they said. The memory of a good teacher or a good student was "like a well-plastered cistern which never loses a drop." There may well have also been a hesitation among the Jews to writing things down

because, if a thing was written, it seemed in a way to challenge the authority of Scripture, and so Scripture tended to be the only thing that was written and so all other teaching was passed down by word of mouth. The *Mishnah* is what we might call the commentary on and the expansion of the laws of the Old Testament. It is the application of the written laws of the Old Testament to particular cases. It was never written down at all until the third century A.D., and, when it was written down, even a summary account of it today in English translation makes a book of over eight hundred pages. All this was carried in the memory of the rabbis. The written word did not have in the ancient world the place that it has today. Papias, who was one of the great collectors of information in the early church wrote: "I did not think that what was to be gotten from books would profit me as much as what came from the living and abiding voice" (quoted, Eusebius, *The Ecclesiastical History* 3:39.4). The first age of the church was not a literary age in anything like the sense in which modern ages became literary, after printing was invented. At least in the East, where Christianity originated, it was much more natural to transmit knowledge and teaching by word of mouth than on the printed page.

2. There was further the fact that Christianity made its first impact on the poorer and the more uncultured classes. "Consider your call, brethren," Paul writes to the Corinthians, "not many of you were wise according to worldly standards, not many were powerful, not many were of noble birth" (1 Corinthians 1:26). It was indeed among the poor and the underprivileged and the slaves that the Christian message made its first main impact.

Early in the third century a pagan philosopher called Celsus made an attack on Christianity. He attacked it on the ground that it appealed only to the poor and the ignorant and the uncultured. He says that the attitude and the invitation of the Christians is: "Let no one cultured draw near, none wise, none sensible, for all that kind of thing we count evil; but, if any man is ignorant, if any man is wanting in sense and culture, if any man is a fool, let him come boldly. . . . It is only the simpletons, the ignoble, the senseless, slaves, and womenfolk and children whom they wish to persuade, or can persuade" (Origen, *Against Celsus* 3.44). In its early days the Christian community was neither a book-reading nor a book-producing community.

3. There were, as we shall see, methods of book production

which foreshadowed mass production. But where was market for Christian books?

Writing materials were not cheap. The writing substance which was made from the papyrus plant was produced in sheets measuring the equivalent of eight by ten inches. One sheet cost at the cheapest the equivalent of five cents per sheet, and in the best quality range it cost twenty cents per sheet. And this has to be evaluated in the light of the fact that the average wage of a working-man was about eight cents per day. In other words, it would cost more than a day's wage to buy a single sheet of the best papyrus. Very few people are going to be able to afford books made of papyrus which cost that kind of figure.

Nor was the process of expert copying cheap, as we have seen. Clearly the cost would be well beyond the reach of most Christians and even of most Christian churches. The very expense of book production tended to delay the formation of anything like a Christian literature.

4. So long as the original apostles continued to live, there was little demand for written books. The apostles and their immediate associates were the living books on which the Christian message was written. They were the eyewitnesses, and so long as they lived, books were not necessary.

5. It may well be that the factor which most of all discouraged the production of books was the belief in the imminence of the Second Coming. We have only to read a chapter like 1 Corinthians 7, where in the light of the short time before the end, as they then expected, Paul discourages marriage in a world which is hastening, as was thought, to its end. If the Second Coming was just round the corner, there was neither the time nor the reason to write books in a world in which the end was due to come at any moment.

These were the main factors which delayed the formation of a Christian literature; but inevitably there came a time when literature was a necessity.

1. The time when the story was passed down by word of mouth was bound to come to an end with the death of the apostles and of those who had been eyewitnesses. By A.D. 70 of the original apostles probably only John was left alive. The story had therefore to be set down. In the nature of things the written word had to take the place of "the living and abiding voice." Eusebius quotes Irenaeus' account of how the Gospels were written. Irenaeus says that after the death of Peter and Paul,

...k, the disciple and interpreter of Peter, transmitted to us in
...ting those things which Peter had preached; and Luke, the
...tendant of Paul, recorded in a book the gospel which Paul had
declared" (*Against Heresies* 3.1.1; quoted by Eusebius, *The
Ecclesiastical History* 5.8.2, 3). The idea is that the written record
was meant to take the place of the living voice. The age of the
eyewitness had to come to an end; the time of the written record
had come.

2. When Christianity went out of Palestine into the larger
world, and particularly when Christianity made contact with
Roman culture and civilization, it entered a society which was
literate and literary, a society in which the book was part of life.
Rome had its bookshops, with the pillars covered with
advertisements for the latest books, and these bookshops were
not only shops; they were the meeting places of cultured society.
In Rome the publishers produced books by slave labor. What
happened was that fifty or a hundred slaves would write to
dictation. Of course, mistakes were made, but by this mass
dictation books could be copied and produced quickly and
cheaply. The first book of Martial has one hundred and
nineteen epigrams in about seven hundred lines of verse, and
copied thus it sold for five *denarii,* which was the equivalent of
about fifty cents. Once Christianity left Palestine and went out
into the world of culture and literature, it went out to a world
which knew all about books, and where the Christian story
would soon be written down.

3. From the beginning Christianity was a missionary religion.
It was obvious that with a world to evangelize, the missionaries
could not stay for any length of time in any one place. It was
therefore necessary to leave a written record of the story they
had told with the new converts in each place. To this day one of
the first tasks of the missionary is to produce a written record of
the Christian story, even if it involves the invention of an
alphabet to do so. A missionary religion is almost obliged to be a
literary religion.

4. As the church grew and developed, there came into the
church people with strange, and even dangerous, ideas. In
other words, it was not long before heresies developed. And in
that situation the church needed some "official" book, some
standard account of the life and teaching of Jesus. It was
precisely such that the New Testament supplied, especially in
the Gospels.

5. We saw that one of the factors which delayed the production of a Christian literature was the supposed imminence of the Second Coming. But the Second Coming was delayed, and the church began to see that it was living in a more or less permanent situation, and in a situation like that a written literature was no longer an irrelevance but a necessity.

In the nature of things it became necessary for the church to produce a Christian literature.

When we have reached this stage in our thinking about the Gospels, a question arises. We have seen that there was considerable delay in the production of a written Gospel. If Jesus died round about A.D. 30 and if the first written Gospel did not emerge until some time between A.D. 65 and 70, what was happening in that thirty-five to forty years when there was no official written account of the life and teaching of Jesus? Is it possible that within this period the story of the life of Jesus and the account of his teaching grew less and less accurate, and more and more a matter of invention? From the point of view of the twentieth century that is a natural question to ask. But in the first century things were very different.

In the first place the ancient memory was much more retentive than the modern memory. It had to be. It may well be said that the printed book, especially when the book is cheap or readily available, has tended to kill the memory. In the ancient days, if a person wanted to retain some story, or some set of facts, he had to do it by memorizing, because books were scarce and expensive. Xenophon tells of Niceratus, "My father," said Niceratus, "was anxious to see me develop into a good man, and as a means to this end he compelled me to memorise all Homer: and so even now I can repeat the whole *Iliad* and *Odyssey* by heart" (*Symposium* 3.6). The *Iliad* and the *Odyssey* each contain twenty-four books, and a book will average about five hundred lines, and this feat of memorization was something that many a Greek boy achieved as part of the education of a cultured man. Nowadays, when we want to enjoy or to refer to a passage, we look it up in a printed book; in the ancient days, when there were few or no books to look up, men carried things in their memories. There was no real fear of the story getting lost or becoming distorted in a day when the memory was strong.

But there was another process operating. There is a necessary corollary to the retentive memory. When things have to be remembered, they tend to become stereotyped. A story comes to be told always in exactly the same way. This process can be seen in the way in which children regard stories. When a child knows and loves a story, it must be told to him always in exactly the same way; he will not accept any deviation from the form of the story which he knows and loves.

So the gospel stories became stereotyped into certain *forms;* and in fairly recent years there has arisen a form of study of the Gospels called Form Criticism, which has made it its objective to find out the *forms* in which the gospel tradition circulated before it came to be set down in the shape of the written Gospels. Those who have studied these matters have identified five different kinds of forms in which the stories are stereotyped.

1. There are what are called paradigms or apothegms or pronouncement stories. These are pieces of tradition whose one reason for existing is that they are intended to preserve a saying of Jesus. The story is not important; the details are few; the one important thing is the saying. To take two examples—the story in Mark 2:23-28 exists simply to enshrine the saying of Jesus: "The sabbath was made for man, not man for the sabbath; so the Son of man is lord even of the sabbath." The story in Matthew 9:10-13 exists to preserve the saying of Jesus: "I came not to call the righteous, but sinners." These stories exist, not for the sake of the story, but for the sake of the saying. The saying is the jewel of which the story is the casket.

2. There are stories which are called tales or novellen. These are stories which tell of some healing deed of Jesus. They all follow the same pattern. There is first a statement of the illness; second, an account of the cure; third, a statement of the consequence of the cure. To take a very simple example, there is the story of the cure of Peter's mother-in-law (Mark 1:29-31). There are:

(a) The statement of the illness—"Now Simon's mother-in-law lay sick with a fever."

(b) The account of the cure—"He came and took her by the hand and lifted her up, and the fever left her."

(c) The consequence or result—"And she served them."

Nearly all of Jesus' miracles are told in this pattern. This is the stereotype which was fixed long before the story was written down.

3. There are sayings. Sayings are epigrammatic and memorable sayings of Jesus which have no context. The pronouncement stories with which we began all arise from an

incident; the sayings are detached sayings of Jesus. The Sermon on the Mount is almost entirely composed of such sayings.

4. We now come to two words which in this connection are used in a technical sense. There are *legends*. In this sense and usage the word *legend* does not make any kind of suggestion about whether or not the event in question actually took place. A legend is a story, told about some holy or famous man or place, and told for religious or moral purposes. In that sense the birth and infancy stories about Jesus are legends.

5. There are *myths*. Once again we must remember that this word *myth* does not express an advance verdict as to whether or not the story is true in fact. The Greeks used the word *muthos* to describe any story which told some story about heavenly and eternal things in terms of things of earth and time. In this sense the temptation story and the transfiguraion story (Matthew 4:1-11; 17:2-8) are myths because they bring on to the scene heavenly and eternal figures in circumstances of space and time.

It was in these forms that the gospel stories were quickly stereotyped in the time between the earthly life of Jesus and the writing down of the Gospels as we now have them. And there is another thing to note which is of the greatest importance. These stories were repeated over and over again for one purpose—for preaching and for the instruction of those entering the Christian community. The importance of this is that these stories were therefore never what we might call private property; they were always public possessions. If there was a change in the telling, the audience would at once ask why. They were not stories told once; they were told again and again and again. The check on them was not simply the memory of the teller; the check on them was the memory of the Christian church. They were not simply the product of one man; they did not depend on any one man's memory. From the beginning they were the possession of the community; they were the material which preachers and teachers continually used, and to which groups of Christians continually listened. The possibility of distortion or falsification is very much reduced, when the story is being continually repeated not only to individuals but also to groups. The guarantor of the truth of any story is not any individual; the guarantor is the united witness of the church.

This leads us to note one more very important fact about the Gospels. The Gospels are not primarily historical documents;

they are not intended to be regarded as biographies of Jesus. They are in fact the preaching material of the early church. John tells us the aim of his Gospel: "These are written that you may believe that Jesus is the Christ, the Son of God, and that believing you may have life in his name" (John 20:30). The aim is not to write a life of Jesus. Many of the things that we would look for in a biography are not there. There is, for instance, no description of what Jesus looked like. It is impossible to construct a timetable of the life of Jesus from the Gospels.

It has been said that there are two ways of writing a story. You may follow the story from day to day and from hour to hour and from event to event in strict chronological order, trying to make the record as complete as possible, and trying to leave nothing out. Or, you may take a series of significant incidents and episodes and use them as windows to see into the mind and the heart of the person you are seeking to know. It is the second method that the gospel writers use. They make no attempt to follow Jesus from place to place and day to day. They take a series of things he said and did to open a series of windows through which we catch glimpses of his mind and heart. It is the difference between a photograph and a portrait. A photograph shows us the subject reproduced in every detail; a portrait seizes on the special characteristics of the person being painted and brings them out. A photograph reproduces in every detail what the person looks like externally; a portrait tries to reveal his inner character and mind and heart. The Gospels are not biographies; they are not photographs. They are attempts to show the mind and the heart and the character of Jesus; and they make this attempt, not simply as matter of interest, and not simply as a contribution to history, but so that those who read may see the mind of God in Jesus. The Gospels are not simply descriptions of Jesus; they are invitations to believe in him as the Son of God.

We have looked at the Letters of Paul, and we have looked at the Gospels. There were other letters in the New Testament also—the Letters of James and Peter and Jude and John. And we have looked at the Gospels, and we have seen what they are meant to be.

Between the Gospels and the letters there comes the book of Acts. It could be argued that Acts is the most important single book in the New Testament, for without it we would know nothing about the history of the early church except what we

could guess and deduce from the letters. Even if we lost t.
the Gospels, we would still have one left, and we would still
some kind of portrait of Jesus; but, if Acts had been lost,
history of the early church would have been shrouded in entir
darkness. It is misleading to call the book *The Acts of the Apostles*.
The only apostles mentioned are James, whose death is given in
one sentence (Acts 12:2). Peter, John, who is always with Peter
and who never himself speaks, and Paul. It is better to call the
book *Acts of Apostolic Men*. In the Greek title there is no *the* before
either Acts or Apostles. The book does not attempt to give a
comprehensive account. What it does do is to open a series of
windows through which significant events in the history of the
early church may be seen.

Acts does three things. First, it tells the story of the expansion
of the church, of how, as Jesus gave his orders, the message
went out from Jerusalem, to Judaea and to Samaria and to the
ends of the earth (Acts 1:8). Second, it tells how this astonishing
crusade began with no more than one hundred and twenty
people (Acts 1:15), and how it was the work of the Spirit (Acts
1:8). The first great story is the story of Pentecost (Acts 2), when
the Holy Spirit came. Thereafter it is the Holy Spirit who
dictates every outgoing movement of the Christian church. It
was the Holy Spirit who instructed Philip to approach the
Ethiopian (Acts 8:29); who told Peter to welcome the
deputation from Cornelius (Acts 10:19); who was responsible
for the dispatch of Paul and Barnabas from Antioch on the first
missionary journey (Acts 13:2); who guided the church into
receiving the Gentiles in its membership (Acts 15:28); who
guided Paul's steps from Asia Minor to Europe (Acts 16:7). Acts
is in reality the book of the acts of the Holy Spirit.

Third, Acts tells us of the message of the early church. In it we
have the summaries of speeches by Peter (2:14-36; 3:12-26;
4:8-12; 4:24-30); by Stephen (7:2-53); by Paul (13:16-41;
14:15-17; 17:22-31). There is no reason to doubt that, though
these are not verbatim reports, they do give the substance of
what early Christian sermons were about.

From them we learn the essence of the early Christian
message.

1. The new age has dawned, and it has dawned through the
life, death, and resurrection of Jesus Christ.

2. Jesus' life and all that happened to him, and especially his
death and resurrection, are the fulfilment of prophecy.

will come again to judge the living and the dead.
herefore repent and receive forgiveness and the gift of
Holy Spirit.

5. He who will not repent will reap the consequences of his refusal.

One thing specially interests us about these speeches. The early Christian preachers never failed to mention the Resurrection. The Resurrection, as it has been put, was "the star in the firmament of early Christianity." And—very surprisingly—these early sermons do not connect the death of Jesus with the forgiveness of sins. The early Church was dominated by the resurrection faith, and by the experience of the Holy Spirit. It had not yet become, what W. D. Davies has called, cross conscious. The cruciality of the cross, as P. T. Forsyth called it, and the interpretation of the cross had to wait for the great mind and heart of Paul.

There is one book in the New Testament which is neither a letter nor a gospel, and it is one of the most puzzling books in the New Testament. It is the book which we call the Revelation, or the Apocalypse. Although it is so strange a book to us, and although it is the only book of its kind in the New Testament, it is in fact a specimen of a kind of book which was very common in the days when the New Testament books were being written.

The Jews divided all time into two ages. There was this present age, and, as they saw it, this present age is wholly bad; it is so bad that it cannot be reformed; it is fit only to be destroyed. Contrasted with this there is the age which is to come, and as they believed, the age which is to come is the golden age of God, when everything will be as God meant it to be, and when the good will enter into their joy and the evil into their destruction. The question is, how was the one age to turn into the other? How was the evil of this present age to become the glory of the age which is to come? By the time of the New Testament, the Jews were sure that this change could never come about by human means; it could not come about by any process of reformation. It could come about only by the total destruction of this present age, and the birth of a new age which would be the age of God. How then would the change take place? They believed that it would take place at the Day of the Lord. The Day of the Lord would be a time when the present world and all that is in it would disintegrate and be destroyed, when there would be a last and final judgment, and when there would arise out of

the chaos a new world which would be the world or
recreated for the people of God.

So there came into being a whole series of books, each of the
called an apocalypse. The word *apocalypse* literally means "ar.
unveiling." And the aim of these books was to tell of the terrible
events of the last days, of the terror of judgment, and of the
golden age which was to come. In the nature of things these
books were unintelligible except to those who understood the
"code," for the books were seeking to tell of things which no eye
had seen, which no ear had heard, and which had never entered
into the minds of men. Many of these books survive, for the
darker the history of the Jewish people, the harder their fate,
the sorer their subjugation and slavery, the more eagerly they
dreamed of the day when God would invade history, when the
dramatic change would come, and when the new age would
dawn. Mostly these are Jewish books, but our Apocalypse is a
Christian specimen of this kind of literature, and this is why it is
the most difficult book in the New Testament for us to
understand. But it must be remembered that, strange as it is, it is
a specimen of one of the commonest kinds of religious
literature in New Testament times.

So, then, as we have it now, the New Testament is composed
of the Four Gospels, Acts, a series of letters written by Paul,
James, Peter, John, Jude, and others, and one Apocalypse. Most
people would agree that it took somewhere about seventy years
to write. The Letter to the Galatians is probably the earliest book
in it—about A.D. 49—and the Second Letter of Peter is probably
the latest book in it—about A.D. 120; and having been written, as
we have already seen, the New Testament took until A.D. 367 to
assume the form in which we have it today.

There are certain milestones on the way to the completion of
the New Testament at which we must now look. The great steps
in the final definition of the contents of the New Testament
were the result of the mistakes into which certain heretics tried
to lead the church.

The first of these heretics was Marcion. He was a wealthy
shipowner from Sinope on the Black Sea coast, and he came to
Rome about A.D. 140. Marcion was a Gnostic. The Gnostics—from a word meaning "knowledge"—were among the
most dangerous heretics who ever threatened the church. They

...t to explain the existence of sin and evil. Their basic *...mption* was that from the beginning of time there have *...n* two principles—matter and spirit, matter and God. Matter *...as* not created; it, as the Gnostics believed, was a basic substance which was always there. It is the basic material out of which the world was made. The matter was essentially evil, just as spirit is essentially good. This is to say that from the beginning the world is made out of flawed material. That is the explanation of sorrow and sin and suffering and pain. The world is made out of bad stuff. But, if matter is evil, this means that the true God who is spirit and who is altogether good could not have touched it. And this means that the true and good God, who is spirit, cannot have been responsible for creation. What happened, as the Gnostics taught, was that the good God put out a series of emanations or aeons, each one more distant from himself. Each emanation was more ignorant of God, and at the end of the scale there was an emanation who was not only ignorant of God, but also hostile to God; and it was this distant, ignorant, hostile emanation who was the creator of the world. This meant that the Gnostics believed that all created things, including the body, are essentially evil. All matter is bad and only spirit is good.

And then the Gnostics took another step. They held that the creator, the distant, hostile, ignorant emanation is the God of the Old Testament, and the real God, the God of spirit, the true God, is the God of the New Testament. This had one obvious consequence. The Gnostic completely, totally and altogether abandoned and discarded the Old Testament. The Old Testament was the book of the ignorant and hostile God. But it also meant that everything in the New Testament which had anything to do with the God of the Old Testament had to go. So of the Christian books Marcion kept only an expurgated version of Luke's Gospel. But Paul was Marcion's hero, for Marcion misunderstood Paul and thought that Paul's attack on the Law was an attack on the Old Testament, and so Marcion kept the Letters of Paul as his most sacred books. So just as the Old Testament consisted of the Law and the Prophets, Marcion's Christian book consisted of the Gospel—Luke—and the Apostle—Paul. Clearly, this was something to which the church had to offer an answer.

Marcion's attack left the church with two obligations. First, the church had to define its attitude to the Old Testament,

which Marcion wished completely to discard, and it had als
make up its mind just what books composed the N.
Testament. The church affirmed its faith in the Old Testamen.
it had no intention of jettisoning it. And there are signs that the
church did face up to the task of defining the New Testament.

There exists a list of New Testament books formulated about
A.D. 170. It is called the Muratorian Canon, after the discoverer
of it. It is slightly mutilated at the beginning, but it is easy to see
just what it contained. Its contents were as follows: the Four
Gospels, Matthew, Mark, Luke, John; the Acts of the Apostles;
Paul's Letters, which it enumerates in the unusual order
Corinthians, Ephesians, Philippians, Colossians, Galatians,
Thessalonians, Romans; to these it adds the Pastoral Epistles,
that is, the Letters to Timothy and to Titus, and the Letter to
Philemon; it includes the Letter of Jude and the First and
Second Letters of John; and the Revelation. It included the
Wisdom of Solomon, and—with a doubt—a second Apocalypse,
the Apocalypse of Peter. The one surprise is the omission of
First Peter. The other books which are omitted—James, Second
Peter, Third John, Hebrews—are the books which took longest
to make their place in the Canon of the New Testament
unquestioned and secure. So we can see that toward the end of
the second century the New Testament is well on the way to
being in the form which it finally took.

For the moment we must turn aside from the story of the final
formation of the New Testament to another question. How did
the process of writing the New Testament come to an end? Why
and when did the Christian church come to the conclusion that
no more New Testament books could be written, or, to put it
more accurately, when did the church decide, and why, that the
quota of sacred books was complete and not to be added to any
more?

This too happened under the influence of a heretic. Some
time toward the end of the second century a man called
Montanus appeared on the scene. Montanus felt that the
original standards of the church had been lowered. He
remembered that Jesus had said that the Spirit would come to
the church, and bring the church fresh truth and fresh
strength. As the Fourth Gospel put it, Jesus had said: "I have yet
many things to say to you, but you cannot bear them now. When
the Spirit of truth comes, he will guide you into all the truth. . . .
He will take what is mine and declare it to you" (John 16:12-14).

...s had promised that the Holy Spirit, the Paraclete, would ...ne, and would, as it were, develop and complete his message. ...hat happened was that Montanus arrived on the scene and claimed that he in fact was the promised Paraclete and that he proposed to give to men the new revelation which Jesus had promised.

This indeed presented the church with a problem; and the church solved it by holding that the revelation of God had been given and completed, and that the days of revelation in the full sense of the term were ended. The church in effect declared that all the sacred books which should be written had been written, and that Scripture was closed. As Tertullian, who later became a Montanist, put it bitterly, the Holy Spirit had been chased into a book. In any event, the Canon of Scripture was regarded as closed. It would never have done, so the church felt, if every now and then someone were to come up with an entirely new revelation. There had to be a time of full revelation by which all other revelations were to be judged. It was decided that that time had come and that no more sacred books could be written. It was not that they had ceased to believe in the revealing power of the Holy Spirit. The difference was that in the first days the Holy Spirit had enabled men to write the sacred books of the Christian religion; in the later days the Holy Spirit enabled men to understand, to interpret and to apply what had been written.

What then was the qualification for a book to gain entry into the church's list of supremely sacred books? The one question asked was whether or not a book was apostolic—that is, whether or not it was written by an actual apostle, or at least by an apostolic man. Thus, as far as the Gospels go, Matthew and John were the work of apostles, and Mark and Luke qualified, because Mark was held to be the disciple and the interpreter of Peter, while Luke was held to have put down in a book the gospel preached by Paul (Irenaeus, *Against Heresies* 3.1.1, 2; Eusebius, *The Ecclesiastical History* 5.8.2). This was in the end why the Letter to the Hebrews was ascribed to Paul. It was known well enough that it was not actually the writing of Paul. As Origen said in the famous sentence: "Who wrote the Letter to the Hebrews only God really knows" (Eusebius, 6.25.11-14). Paul was the great letter writer; the Letter to the Hebrews was so valuable that the church wanted to keep it as one of the sacred books; and so to give it the status it needed it was added to the Letters of Paul.

There was a good reason for making apostolic authorship the standard of acceptance of any book as one of the church's sacred and authoritative books. Christianity is an historical religion. Christianity took its origin and its power from an historical person, Jesus of Nazareth. Therefore the one necessity was an unbroken chain of evidence going right back to him. The world was full of the stories of dying and rising gods. The only way to make it certain that the Christian gospel was not simply another of these stories was to trace it back to someone who could say: "I know that this is true, because with my own eyes I saw it."

This stressing of apostolic authorship had one interesting consequence. On general grounds it seems strange that the church kept four different Gospels. The fact that there were four Gospels could produce embarrassing situations. For instance, the Fourth Gospel has the incident of the cleansing of the temple at the beginning of the ministry of Jesus, and the other three have it at the end. The fact that there are four Gospels often produces problems of harmonization. There was an experiment in harmonizing the Gospels made by a man called Tatian about A.D. 180. Tatian produced the *Diatessaron,* which literally means "through four," and in it he made a harmony of the Gospels in which by a scissors-and-paste method he managed to include almost everything. A fragment of the Diatessaron read like this:

> And the day was Preparation; the Sabbath was dawning (Luke 23:54). And when it was evening, on the Preparation, that is the day before the Sabbath (Matthew 27:57; Mark 15:42), there came up a man, being a member of the council (Matthew 27:57; Luke 23:50), from Arimathaea, a city of Judah, by name Joseph (Matthew 27:57; Luke 23:50), good and righteous, being a disciple of Jesus, but secretly for fear of the Jews (Matthew 27:57; Luke 23:50; John 19:38). And he was looking for the kingdom of God (Luke 23:51). This man had not consented to their purpose (Luke 23:51).

It is true that Tatian's *Diatessaron* was not put together with any great artistry, but one would have expected the Four Gospels to be woven into one narrative. What stopped that was the overwhelming importance of apostolic testimony. The Gospels were all of them the work of apostolic men or of apostles; and it was therefore more important to keep them as they were than to harmonize them. So much so, that on there being four Gospels, Irenaeus could write: "As there are four quarters of the world in which we live, as there are four universal winds, and as the church is scattered all over the earth, and the gospel is the pillar and base of the church and the breath of life, it is likely that it should have four pillars breathing immortality on every side and kindling afresh the life of men. Whence it is evident that the Word, the architect of all things, who sits upon the cherubim and holds all things together, having been made manifest to men, gave us the gospel in a fourfold shape, but held together by one Spirit" (*Against Heresies* 3.11.8). So in the end it came to be argued that it was just as natural that there should be four Gospels as that there should be four points of the compass.

So then the Gospels and the Letters took their place as the books of the church; and that place became secure when they began to be read at the public worship of the church. When, as the years passed on, they became part of every service of the church, they were fully established.

We may complete this story by noting still one other thing. For a time there were certain books whose position was not secure. Two of the great early scholars of the church made investigations about the contents of the Christian Scriptures.

The first was Origen who lived from A.D. 182 to 251. In his time the situation was that the place of the Four Gospels, of the Letters of Paul, including Hebrews, of 1 Peter, 1 John, and the Revelation was undisputed and secure. Origen goes on to say that Peter may have left another letter, but that this was doubtful. Second and Third John he knew but not everyone, he said, considered them genuine. And James and Jude he never mentions at all.

The second was Eusebius of Caesarea, the great church historian who lived from A.D. 270 to 330. He divided the books of the church into three classes—the universally accepted, the disputed, and the spurious. The universally accepted are the Four Gospels, Acts, the Letters of Paul, including Hebrews, 1 John, and 1 Peter. The Revelation hovered between the universally accepted and the disputed. The disputed books are James, Jude, 2 Peter, and 2 and 3 John. He says that 2 Peter is not generally accepted, but that because it has been found profitable by many it may well be Scripture. He says that many regard the Letter of James as spurious, and that very few of the

early writers of the church have ever mentioned it. The list
Eusebius is to all intents and purposes the same as that
Origen.

So finally we come to the last stage. The first time, as we began
by saying, that we find the books of the New Testament listed
exactly as we have them today is in the Easter Letter of
Athanasius to his people in A.D. 367, and it marks such an epoch
that the relevant section must be quoted in full:

> There must be no hesitation to state again the books of the New
> Testament, for they are these: Four Gospels, according to Matthew,
> according to Mark, according to Luke and according to John.
> Further, after these, also the Acts of the Apostles, and the seven
> so-called Catholic Epistles of the Apostles, as follows: one of James,
> but two of Peter, then three of John, and after these one of Jude; in
> addition to these there are fourteen Epistles of the apostle Paul put
> down in the following order: the first to the Romans, then two to the
> Corinthians, and after these the Epistles to the Galatians, and then to
> the Ephesians: further, the Epistles to the Philippians and to the
> Colossians and two to the Thessalonians, and the Epistle to the
> Hebrews. And next two Letters to Timothy, but one to Titus, and the
> last one to Philemon. Moreover also, the Apocalypse of John.

Here for the first time is the complete New Testament as we
know it.

So then by 367 the New Testament was completed and the
canon was closed. There was never again to be any variation in
it. It is, however, worthwhile to see what Luther has to say on the
subject. To us nowadays the attitude of the Reformers seems
quite astonishingly free and radical. They claimed a sovereign
liberty in regard to the place they gave to certain books. Luther
had only one touchstone, and he expressed it with his usual
vivid violence: "That which does not teach Christ is not
apostolic," though Peter or Paul should have said it; on the
contrary, that which does preach Christ is apostolic, even if it
should come from Judas, Annas, Herod, or Pilate.

There were certain books to which Luther gave a supreme
place, and certain books to which he gave a secondary place.
There are twenty-seven books in the New Testament. On the
title page of his own translation of the New Testament Luther
printed and numbered twenty-three of them; then at the end in
a little group of their own, indented and not numbered, he
placed James, Hebrews, Jude, and the Revelation. James, he

..., was "an epistle of straw; for it has nothing of the nature of .e gospel about it." It teaches justification by works; it contradicts Paul; and it has nothing to say about the life and the death and the resurrection of Jesus, and about the Holy Spirit. Hebrews in three places in chapters 6, 10, 12, says that there can be no repentance after baptism, and this, says Luther, is in flat contradiction to the teaching of the Gospels and of Paul. Jude is no more than an extract from 2 Peter; it is in fact included very largely in 2 Peter. As for the Revelation, Luther said of it: "I hold it to be neither apostolic nor prophetic. . . . My spirit cannot acquiesce in the book." He went on to say: "I abide by the books which present Christ pure and clear. . . . After all, in it Christ is neither taught nor acknowledged."

Luther's standards were completely clear. In his Preface to the New Testament he writes—and we must quote the passage in full:

> John's Gospel and St. Paul's epistles, especially that to the Romans, and St. Peter's first Epistle are the true kernel and marrow of all the books. . . .
>
> In them you find not many works and miracles of Christ described, but you do find it depicted, in masterly fashion, how faith in Christ overcomes sin, death and hell, and gives life, righteousness and salvation. This is the real nature of the Gospel. . . . If I had to do without one or the other—either the works or the preaching of Christ—I would rather do without his works than his preaching; for the works do not help me, but his words give life, as he himself says. . . . Now John writes very little about the works of Christ, but very much about his preaching; therefore John's Gospel is the one, tender, true, chief Gospel, far, far, to be preferred to the other three and placed high above them. So too the Epistles of St. Paul and St. Peter far surpass the other three Gospels—Matthew, Mark and Luke.
>
> In a word, John's Gospel and his First Epistle, St. Paul's Epistles, especially Romans, Galatians, and Ephesians, and St. Peter's First Epistle are the books that show you Christ and teach you all that it is necessary and good for you to know, even though you were never to see or hear any other book or doctrine.

Luther has no hesitation in drawing distinctions between the books of the New Testament. He makes it clear that this preference is a personal thing. At the end of his Introduction to James he writes: "Therefore, I cannot put him among the chief books, though I would not thereby prevent anyone from putting him where he pleases and estimating him as he pleases, for there are many good things in him."

For Luther all the New Testament books were h...
within the New Testament there was a special Holy of Ho...
books where above all Jesus Christ is to be encountered.

This then is the story of how the New Testament came to b...
what it is today, and although to Luther and others there have
always been some books which are dearer and more precious
than others, for the last sixteen hundred years no book has been
added and no book has been taken away.

The Apocrypha

We have now studied the story of the making of the Old Testament and the making of the New Testament. But there is still another group of books at which we must look. These books form what is known as the Apocrypha. These books are often bound in with the Old and the New Testament in one composite volume. We cannot say that they are universally regarded as part of the Bible as the Old and New Testaments are. But we certainly cannot pass them over in silence, because for the Roman Catholic Church these books are an integral part of the Bible and for the Anglican Church they have a considerable share in the church's lectionary, and they are regarded as at least sacred and profitable books.

We must begin by looking at the meaning of the word *Apocrypha*. The word is a Greek neuter plural from the word *apokruphon,* and it means things which ought to be kept secret and hidden away. This word is applied to three different kinds of books or information.

1. It was applied to books which were too difficult, too sacred, or too holy for common use. As we have seen, 2 Esdras (4 Ezra) 14:19-48 has the story of how Ezra restored the sacred books when they had been burned and destroyed in the days of the exile. The story is legendary, but it does show the place that Ezra had in popular thought, and it does illustrate the kind of thing meant by this first use of the word *apokrupha.*

It was Ezra's task to rewrite the lost Law. He was told to take five scribes who were trained to write rapidly. They proceeded to an open field. There Ezra was given a cup. "It was full of something like water, but its color was like fire." Ezra drank it and began to dictate. The dictation went on for forty days, during which ninety-four books were dictated and written. Then the Most High said to Ezra: "Make public the twenty-four books that you wrote first and let the worthy and the unworthy read them; but keep the seventy that were written last, in order to give them to the wise among your people. For in them is the spring of understanding, the fountain of wisdom, and the river of knowledge." The twenty-four books were the books of the

Old Testament. What the others were we cannot te
point is that the idea of books to be kept secret fr
ordinary person was a familiar enough idea. So then the
meaning of the word *apocrypha* is "secret," because too sac
and too lofty for ordinary use.

2. There is a modren use of the word *apocryphal* which is the
very opposite of that. If nowadays we describe a story as
apocryphal, we mean that it is fictitious. An apocryphal story is
the opposite of a true story. The word is used to describe the
legendary tales which often gather round distinguished people.
In this sense the word apocryphal describes something inferior
rather than something superior.

3. But when the word *apocrypha* is used to describe these books
of which we are at present thinking, the main meaning of it is
that the books in question are not to be read in public and at
public worship, but there is no objection to their being read
privately at home for instruction and profit. This is the
prevailing Protestant use of the word. The Roman Catholic
Church does not call these books The Apocrypha at all. For it
they are fully and truly Scripture. But, generally speaking, for
the Protestant Church the term denotes a book of secondary
significance, admittedly useful, but not to be ranked with books
which are unquestionably Scripture.

First, then, what are the books which are included among the
Apocrypha? These books number fourteen or fifteen:

1 Esdras
2 Esdras (sometimes referred to as 4 Ezra)
Tobit
Judith
The Additions to the Book of Esther
The Wisdom of Solomon
Ecclesiasticus, or the Wisdom of Jesus the Son of Sirach
Baruch
The Letter of Jeremiah
The Prayer of Azariah and the Song of the Three Young Men
Susanna
Bel and the Dragon
The Prayer of Manasseh
The First Book of the Maccabees
The Second Book of the Maccabees

...mprises fifteen books; but sometimes the Letter of
...n is included as the last chapter of Baruch, and then the
...er becomes fourteen.

These fifteen books fall into various types and classifications.
1. There are books which are additions to books which are
already in the Old Testament.

There are the Additions to Esther. In the Book of Esther as it
stands in the Old Testament, there is not one single mention of
the name of God, and there is not one single instance of anyone
at prayer. All the additions except one mention the name of
God, and one mentions the name of God no fewer than nine
times in nine verses, while in another of the additions both
Esther and Mordecai are shown at prayer. These additions are
designed to supply what was wanting in the original book.

The Prayer of Azariah and the Song of the Three Young
Men, Susanna and Bel and the Dragon are all additions to
Daniel. Azariah is the Hebrew name of Abed-nego, and the
Prayer and the Song are put into the mouths of the three young
men in the burning fiery furnace. The Prayer is one of the great
praising prayers of the world. Here are some verses from it:

Bless the Lord, sun and moon,
   sing praise to him,
      and highly exalt him for ever.
Bless the Lord, stars of heaven,
   sing praise to him,
      and highly exalt him for ever.
Bless the Lord, all rain and dew,
   sing praise to him,
      and highly exalt him for ever.
Bless the Lord, all winds,
   sing praise to him,
      and highly exalt him for ever.
Bless the Lord, fire and heat,
   sing praise to him,
      and highly exalt him for ever.
Bless the Lord, winter cold and summer heat,
   sing praise to him,
      and highly exalt him for ever.
Bless the Lord, dews and snows,
   sing praise to him,
      and highly exalt his name for ever.
Bless the Lord, nights and days,

sing praise to him,
and highly exalt his name for ever.
Bless the Lord, light and darkness,
sing praise to him,
and highly exalt his name for ever.
Bless the Lord, ice and cold,
sing praise to him,
and highly exalt his name for ever.
Bless the Lord, frosts and snows,
sing praise to him,
and highly exalt his name for ever.
Bless the Lord, lightnings and clouds,
sing praise to him,
and highly exalt his name for ever.
Let the earth bless the Lord;
let it sing praise to him,
and highly exalt his name for ever.

The other two additional pieces to Daniel have a fame all their own, for they are designed to show the wisdom of Daniel, and they are perhaps the two earliest detective stories in the literature of the world. Dorothy Sayers included them at the beginning of her *Omnibus of Crime* published in 1929.

Susanna is the story of a beautiful and virtuous woman. Two Jewish elders conceived a guilty passion for her. On one summer day Susanna informed her maids that she wished to bathe in the pool in her garden. The two elders concealed themselves in the garden and, while Susanna was bathing sprang out, and sought to seduce her. She refused their requests; they said that, if she did not yield to them, they would say that they had discovered her in the garden in the arms of a lover. She refused them. They made their charges, and, since they were known and respected elders, Susanna was found guilty. Daniel appeared and asked for a retrial, which was granted. Daniel examined each of the elders separately. He asked each of them the same question. "Under what kind of tree did you see Susanna in the embrace of her lover?" "A mastic tree," the first said. "An evergreen oak," the second said. It was seen at once that their story was fictitious, and Susanna was vindicated. So the story is an exercise in cross-examination.

There are two stories in Bel and the Dragon. Bel was the great god of the Babylonians. Daniel insisted to the king that Bel was nothing but a lifeless idol. "How then," demanded the king, "does he consume the vast amount of food that is left in the for him each night?" For every night there were left in

emple twelve bushels of fine flour, forty sheep, and fifty

ons of wine. Daniel knew that the priests had an underground

ntrance into the temple. So the offerings were put into the
temple, and the doors were locked, and the building was left for
the night. But unknown to anyone Daniel had covered the floor of
the temple with fine powdered ash. Sure enough, in the morning
all the food was gone; and the priests clamored for Daniel's death.
But Daniel told the king to look at the floor of the temple, and
there in the ash were the crowded footprints of men, women and
children, and the deception of the priests was exposed, and Bel
forever discredited.

No doubt these stories were never meant to be taken as
history. They are what one writer has called moralistic novels,
but to this day they remain among the great short stories of the
world's literature.

2. There are two magnificent stories on the list. There is
Tobit, the charming story of the journey of Tobias in the
company of Raphael the angel, who disguised himself as a man,
and with the little dog. And there is the bloodthirsty thriller of
Judith, who in the days of her country's peril, made her way into
the hostile camp, deceived Holofernes the Assyrian general into
thinking that he might have his way with her, made him blind
drunk, cut off his head, and brought it home in a bag—one of
the great scenarios of the world!

Maybe Shakespeare knew and loved these stories, for he
called his daughters Susanna and Judith!

3. There are two long didactic books. They belong to what is
called the Wisdom Literature. The word *wisdom* used of that
kind of literature does not refer to philosophic and intellectual
wisdom; it refers to the practical wisdom which enables a man to
live a good life both in the eyes of men and the sight of God. The
Wisdom of Solomon was written sometime late in the first
century B.C. or in the first century A.D. It is a long book with some
magnificent passages in it. We choose one which brings comfort
to face death to those in trouble:

> The souls of the righteous are in the hand of God,
> and no torment will ever touch them.
> In the eyes of the foolish they seemed to have died,
> and their departure was thought to be an affliction,
> and their going from us to be their destruction;
> but they are at peace.

For though in the sight of men they were punished,
their hope is full of immortality.
Having been disciplined a little, they will receive great good, because
God tested them and found them worthy of himself. (3:1-5)

The book was attributed to Solomon, because Solomon was the
man whose name above all was connected with true wisdom.

The other of the great Wisdom books of the Apocrypha is
entitled The Wisdom of Jesus the Son of Sirach, or, to call it by
its better known name, Ecclesiasticus. It was originally written in
Hebrew about 180 B.C., and about fifty years later the grandson
of the original writer took it to Egypt and translated it into
Greek.

There are many famous passages in Ecclesiasticus, of which
perhaps the most famous of all is the long section in praise of
famous men (chapters 44–50). Especially famous is the
introduction to that section (44:1-15).

Let us now praise famous men,
and our fathers in their generations.
The Lord apportioned to them great glory,
his majesty from the beginning.
There were those who ruled in their kingdoms,
and were men renowned for their power,
giving counsel by their understanding,
and proclaiming prophecies;
leaders of the people in their deliberations
and in understanding of learning for the people,
wise in their words of instruction;
those who composed musical tunes,
and set forth verses in writing . . .
All these were honoured in their generations,
and were the glory of their times.
There are some of them who have left a name,
so that men declare their praise.
And there are some who have no memorial,
who have perished as though they had not lived . . .
Their bodies were buried in peace,
and their name lives to all generations.
People will declare their wisdom,
and the congregation proclaims their praise.

It is in Ecclesiasticus that there is the famous tribute to doctors
(38:1-14):

Honour the physician with the honour due him,
according to your need of him,
for the Lord created him;
for healing comes from the Most High,
and he will receive a gift from the king.
The skill of the physician lifts up his head,
and in the presence of great men he is admired.
The Lord created medicines from the earth,
and a sensible man will not despise them . . .
By them he heals and takes away pain;
the pharmacist makes of them a compound.
His works will never be finished;
and from him health is upon the face of the earth . . .
There is a time when success lies in the hands of physicians,
for they too will pray to the Lord
that he should grant them success in diagnosis
and in healing, for the sake of preserving life.

There is still another famous passage in which Sirach holds that only the man of leisure can ever become a great scholar and teacher, and that wisdom is not possible for the workers of the world. But, having said that, he pays the workers a great tribute (38:31-34):

All these rely upon their hands,
and each is skilful in his own work.
Without them a city cannot be established,
and men can neither sojourn nor live there.
Yet they are not sought out for the council of the people,
nor do they attain eminence in the public assembly.
They do not sit in the judge's seat,
nor do they understand the sentence of judgment;
they cannot expound discipline or judgment,
and they are not found using proverbs.
But they keep stable the fabric of the world,
and their prayer is in the practice of their trade.

The Wisdom of Solomon and Ecclesiasticus are two very great books. From its earliest days the church knew and valued them, and urged its members to read them. There are not a few who would gladly see them in the Canon of Scripture.

4. There are certain books in the Apocrypha which have to do with historical events. There is 1 Esdras, which does no more than retrace the ground covered in part of 2 Chronicles and in Ezra and Nehemiah. It has only one additional passage in it, and

that the origin of a famous proverbial saying. As the AV has it, "Great is Truth and mighty above all things."

The other two historical books are 1 and 2 Maccabees. These are important because in their different ways they tell the story of the famous fight for freedom in which Judas Maccabaeus is the most famous name. Of 1 Maccabees Martin Luther said that it was "not unworthy to be reckoned among the books of Scripture."

5. There is one book which we might call devotional. This is The Prayer of Manasseh. Manasseh, as the Hebrew historian saw him, was one of the worst of the kings (2 Kings 21:1-18; 2 Chronicles 33:1-20). He reigned for fifty-five years; he was guilty of "the abominable practices" of the heathen nations of the land. He built altars to Baal; he worshiped "the host of heaven"; he offered his son as a sacrifice; he kept mediums and magicians. He set up a graven image of Asherah in the very temple itself, and he shed innocent blood. For this the Babylonians were to be unloosed against Judaea, the temple was to be destroyed and the people were to be banished (2 Kings 24:3). The Chronicler tells us that for a time Manasseh himself was in exile. They "took Manasseh with hooks and bound him with fetters of bronze and brought him to Babylon." There in captivity Manasseh repented of all his evil ways and prayed to God, and God brought him back to Jerusalem. God heard his prayer and received his entreaty (2 Chronicles 33:10-19). The Prayer of Manasseh is supposed to be the prayer that Manasseh prayed in the bitterness of his exile, and the aim of this single-page work is to show that, even for a Manasseh, there is forgiveness, if he repents before God. Here are some verses from it:

> I have sinned, O Lord, I have sinned,
>   and I know my transgressions.
> I earnestly beseech thee,
>   forgive me, O Lord, forgive me!
>   Do not destroy me with my transgressions!
> Do not be angry with me for ever or lay up evil for me;
>   do not condemn me to the depths of the earth.
> For thou, O Lord, art the God of those who repent,
>   and in me thou wilt manifest thy goodness;
> for, unworthy as I am, thou wilt save me in thy great mercy,
>   and I will praise thee continually all the days of my life.
> For all the host of heaven sings thy praise,
>   and thine is the glory for ever. Amen.

Here is the confidence that, if he repents, the worst of sinners can be saved.

6. There are two books which are in the prophetic succession. The first is the book of Baruch, written probably in the first century B.C., and purporting to be written by Baruch the secretary of Jeremiah (Jeremiah 36:4). Sometimes the Letter of Jeremiah is appended to Baruch as a sixth chapter. The Letter of Jeremiah is a scathing indictment of idolatry. It must come from a time when the Jews were tempted and invited to share the idolatrous worship of their neighbors. It is the craftsmen who make the idols. "People take gold and make crowns for the heads of their gods, as they would for a girl who loves ornaments." And sometimes the priests steal the gold, and gold can be spent even in a brothel. The dust of the temple gathers on them, and they have to be cleaned and dusted down. Bats, swallows, birds, and cats sit on them. If they have to be moved they have to be carried, because they have no feet of their own. If you put them down, they tip over and collapse and have to be hoisted up again. "They cannot save a man from death or rescue the weak from the strong. They cannot restore sight to a blind man; they cannot rescue a man who is in distress." The men who manufacture them are dying men—how can they make gods? If the temple goes on fire, the priests can flee and rescue themselves, but the gods can only burn helplessly. They are no better than a scarecrow in a garden.

In this little pamphlet idolatry is blasted with ridicule, which even yet is effective.

7. Lastly, there is one apocalyptic book. This is 2 Esdras, or, as it is sometimes called, 4 Ezra. We have already seen that apocalyptic literature deals with the terrible end-time when this present age and all its evil will be destroyed, and when the Day of the Lord will come, and the new age of God's kingdom will be born. That time is to be a time of complete destruction and of utter disintegration. These apocalyptic books, as we have seen, describe the indescribable, and tell of the things which no eye has seen, no ear has heard, and no mind has conceived. They are unintelligible except to the initiated, and 4 Ezra is no exception. Luther found it so bizarre that, when he translated the Apocrypha, he did not even attempt to translate this book. In his characteristically violent way he said that he threw it into the Elbe!

Second Esdras took a long time in the writing. The basis of it is chapters 3 to 14, which purport to be the record of seven revelations given to Ezra in Babylon. This part was written about A.D. 100. This section was originally written in Aramaic. It was later translated into Greek, except for two or three verses. The version in which it exists is the Latin version. About A.D. 150 an anonymous and unknown Christian writer added chapters 1 and 2 in Greek. And about A.D. 250 still another unknown Christian writer added chapters 15 and 16. It had always been clear that there was some kind of gap between 7:35 and 7:36. In 1874 the missing Latin text of these verses turned up and were inserted into the text.

A brief illustration of the visions of this strange book is taken from chapter 5:

> The sun shall suddenly shine forth at night,
>   and the moon during the day.
> Blood shall drip from wood,
>   and the stone shall utter its voice;
> the peoples shall be troubled,
>   and the stars shall fall.

This is a book which has little or nothing to say to us nowadays.

We have now seen what the Apocrypha are, and we must go on to ask where the books came from, and why their position is doubtful. The answer to the first part of this question is that the books of the Apocrypha appear in the Greek version of the Old Testament, but not in the original Hebrew. The Greek version of the Old Testament is called the Septuagint. In the reign of Ptolemy the Second Philadelphus, which extended from 285 to 246 B.C., the Old Testament was translated into Greek in Egypt. This was the fitting place for that translation to be made, because at that time there were more than a million Jews in Egypt, many of whom had never been in Palestine. These Jews had either forgotten, or had never known, Hebrew. Greek was the language they used. The Septuagint—it is usually designated by the letters LXX, the Latin form of the number 70, which was the number of its translators—is one of the most important books in the world, because it was it which made the Old Testament available to nearly everyone, for everyone knew Greek, and only a few people knew Hebrew. In due time the Septuagint was to be the basis of the first translation of the Old Testament into Latin, and therefore the earliest Latin Old

Testament had the same form as the Greek Old Testament. We will see what happened if we set down side by side, in the order in which they occur, the books of the Old Testament in its Hebrew, Greek, Latin, and English versions.

HEBREW	GREEK SEPTUAGINT	LATIN	ENGLISH
The Law	*The Laws*	*Historical*	Genesis
Genesis	Genesis	*Books*	Exodus
Exodus	Exodus	Genesis	Leviticus
Leviticus	Leviticus	Exodus	Numbers
Numbers	Numbers	Leviticus	Deuteronomy
Deuteronomy	Deuteronomy	Numbers	Joshua
		Deuteronomy	Judges
The Prophets	*The Histories*	Joshua	Ruth
Joshua	Joshua	Judges	1 and 2
Judges	Judges	Ruth	Samuel
1 and 2 Samuel	Ruth	1 and 2 Kings	1 and 2 Kings
1 and 2 Kings	1 and 2 Kings	3 and 4 Kings	1 and 2
Isaiah	(= 1 and 2	1 and 2	Chronicles
Jeremiah	Samuel)	Chronicles	Ezra
Ezekiel	3 and 4 Kings	1 Esdras	Nehemiah
Hosea	(= 1 and 2)	(= Ezra)	Esther
Joel	Kings)	2 Esdras	Job
Amos	1 and 2	(= Nehemiah)	Psalms
Obadiah	Chronicles	Tobit	Proverbs
Jonah	1 Esdras	Judith	Ecclesiastes
Micah	2 Esdras (Ezra,	Esther	Song of
Nahum	Nehemiah)		Solomon
Habakkuk	Esther	*Didactic*	Isaiah
Zephaniah	Judith	*Books*	Jeremiah
Haggai	Tobit	Job	Lamentations
Zechariah	1, 2, 3, 4,	Psalms	Ezekiel
Malachi	Maccabees	Proverbs	Daniel
		Ecclesiastes	Hosea
The Writings	*Poetical*	Song of	Joel
Psalms	*Books*	Solomon	Amos
Proverbs	Psalms	Wisdom	Obadiah
Job	Odes	Ecclesiasticus	Jonah
Song of	Proverbs		Micah
Solomon	Ecclesiastes	*Prophetical*	Nahum
Ruth	Song of	*Books*	Habakkuk
Lamentations	Solomon	Isaiah	Zephaniah
Ecclesiastes	Job	Jeremiah	Haggai
Esther	Wisdom	Lamentations	Zechariah
Daniel	Ecclesiasticus	Baruch	Malachi

Ezra
Nehemiah
1 and 2
  Chronicles

Psalms of
  Solomon

Prophetical
Books
Hosea
Amos
Micah
Joel
Obadiah
Jonah
Nahum
Habakkuk
Zephaniah
Haggai
Zechariah
Malachi
Isaiah
Jeremiah
Baruch
Lamentations
The Letter of
  Jeremiah
Ezekiel
Susanna
Daniel
Bel and the
  Dragon

Ezekiel
Daniel
Hosea
Joel
Amos
Obadiah
Jonah
Micah
Nahum
Habakkuk
Zephaniah
Haggai
Malachi

Books of
Recent
History
1 and 2
  Maccabees

It can be seen at once that the Hebrew, the Greek, the Latin and the English Bible differ widely in the books which they do and do not contain, and just as widely in the order in which they have the books.

From the lists one thing is clear—the Greek Old Testament, the Septuagint, is by far the most inclusive. It includes even books which are not in the official Apocrypha, for example, 3 and 4 Maccabees, the Odes, and the Psalms of Solomon. Why should this be? As we have seen, for the Jews of Palestine the sacred writings comprised twenty-four books and no more; their canon was closed. "If anyone," said the rabbis, "receives more than twenty-four books, he introduces confusion into his house." By the Jewish law it was illegal to carry a burden on the sabbath day, and it was laid down that, if there was a fire in a house, only the twenty-four books could be carried out and no more. On the other hand, the Jews of Alexandria had much wider sympathies. For them, if a book was inspiring, it was inspired. So in the early days there were the two versions of the Old Testament, the limited version of the Palestinian Jews and the inclusive version of the Greek-speaking Jews; and the extra books in the Greek version are the Apocrypha. And since in the early days far more people used the Greek than the Hebrew Old Testament, there was a time when these extra books were very widely received.

Have we then reached a stage at which there were two Old Testaments—a shorter Hebrew one and a larger Greek one? The Apocrypha form quite a considerable unit of material. Bruce Metzger expresses it statistically:

	Books	Chapters	Verses
Old Testament	39	929	23,214
New Testament	27	260	7,959
Apocrypha	14/15	183	6,081

Do we then have an "official" form of the Old Testament which has something between one fifth and one quarter more material in it than the Hebrew Old Testament has?

The answer is yes—and no! Even here at this early stage we are already at a position in which the Apocrypha occupy a curiously elusive position, neither wholly Scripture nor wholly non-Scripture. Certain things have to be noted.

1. There is never any word of an extension of the canon. The Greek writers knew and loved and used the Apocrypha, but they never at any time questioned the Hebrew Canon of Scripture, and they never, as it were, listed any additions to it.

2. The books included and not included in the Septuagint vary to some extent. For instance, 4 Ezra never occurs in the Septuagint, because, as we have seen, it does not exist in its Greek form. The Prayer of Manasseh is sometimes there and sometimes not there. Some manuscripts of the Septuagint contain 3 and 4 Maccabees, and sometimes a psalm numbered Psalm 151. Even the number of the extra books is not strictly fixed.

3. The great Jewish Alexandrian scholar was Philo. It was he who attempted to marry Jewish and Greek thought. He came from the area in which the Septuagint was born, although his work was done much later, just when the New Testament was coming into being. All his work is in the form of commentary on

and exposition of Scripture. Philo knew and valued these extra books, but he never quotes them as Scripture.

4. The writers of the New Testament were all Greek-speaking. Their Bible was not the Hebrew Old Testament; it was the Greek Septuagint. This was what they knew and quoted, but to all intents and purposes they never quote the books of the Apocrypha, and certainly not as Scripture.

Here there is the proof that the books of the Apocrypha occupied a curiously intermediate position, in which they were used and valued, and yet fell short of being in the full sense Scripture. One thing is noticeable about the use of these books, and even it has in it this double slant. As might be expected, we find in the early fathers two attitudes to these books. The fathers who were scholars and who knew Hebrew—and in the early times such scholars were few and far between—generally rejected the Apocrypha as Scripture and adhered to the Hebrew Bible, while the fathers who knew no Hebrew and who knew only Greek or Latin tended to accept the Apocrypha, because they found them bound into their version of the Old Testament. Thus Jerome and Origen, who were among the world's great scholars—Jerome had gone to reside in Palestine in order to learn Hebrew—were clear that the Apocrypha were not part of Scripture, while fathers like Tertullian and Augustine, who knew no Hebrew, accepted the Apocrypha as part of Scripture.

And yet the division was by no means as clear as that. Jerome could and did say, after listing the books in the Hebrew Old Testament: "Whatever is not included in this list is to be classed as apocryphal. Therefore Wisdom, commonly entitled of Solomon, the Book of Jesus the Son of Sirach, Judith, and Tobit . . . are not in the canon." And yet, when it came to the point, at the request of the bishops he translated them and included them in the Vulgate, of which he was the translator and which became, and still is, the Bible of the Roman Catholic Church. As a scholar, Jerome would have banished the books of the Apocrypha; as a churchman he accepted them. As for Augustine, in his work *On Christian Doctrine* he included in the Old Testament Judith, Tobit, 1 and 2 Maccabees, Ecclesiasticus, Wisdom. He agreed with Jerome that they were not in the Hebrew Scriptures and that logically they should not be there, but he was worried about the effect of their exclusion on the minds of simple people who had long used and loved them.

To him ecclesiastical tradition meant more than critical scholarship.

Origen was the same. About A.D. 240 Julius Africanus, the Bishop of Emmaus in Palestine, argued with him that Susanna is not in the Hebrew Bible and should not be regarded as Scripture. No one knew this better than Origen and as a scholar he would agree, but he argued that the Christian church has always accepted these books for edification; he declared that the church was not going to prune its reading to suit the Jews; he said that immemorial tradition was authority enough for reading these books. And he reminded Julius that the Bible itself said that ancient landmarks were not to be removed (Deuteronomy 19:14). There was always a tension between critical scholarship and church tradition and tradition won. Rufinus introduced a distinction between *canonical* books and *ecclesiastical* books, and among the ecclesiastical books he included Wisdom, Ecclesiasticus, Tobit, Judith, and 1 and 2 Maccabees. They were not canonical, but they were books of the church. Jerome introduced still another distinction which stood for a long time, which in fact in some places stands even yet. He said of Ecclesiasticus and Wisdom that they are books which the church reads "for edification of the people, but not for the proving of the doctrines of the church."

So we see that in the early centuries for the Jews there was no question. Only the twenty-four books written in Hebrew were to be regarded as Scripture. In the Greek Old Testament, there were considerably more books. But the extra books in the Greek Old Testament were never quite reckoned as on the same footing as the Hebrew books. The church knew them and the church valued them and the church would not abandon them, but it would not give them the same status as it gave to the Hebrew books of the Jewish Old Testament.

We now come to the place of the Apocrypha in the English Bible. In the earliest of the English Bibles, in Wycliffe's translation, the Apocryphal books appear scattered throughout the Old Testament. This was so because Wycliffe did not translate from the Hebrew; he translated from the Latin Vulgate, and in the Wycliffe Bible the Apocrypha are as in the Latin Bible. But another influence was to weigh even more heavily on the English translators, and was to lead to the Apocrypha being given the position in the printed Bible, which they regularly occupy in the Protestant Bible. Luther's translation of the Bible into German was completed in 1534. It was not the Latin that Luther used; it was the original Greek and Hebrew. So in the Luther German translation the Apocryphal books are segregated into a separate section of the end of the Old Testament and before the New Testament. The section is headed: "APOCRYPHA—that is, books which are not held equal to the Holy Scriptures, and yet are profitable and good to read." Luther did not translate 1 and 2 Esdras (4 Ezra). He said of 2 Esdras (4 Ezra) that he threw it into the Elbe, and in his preface to Baruch he said of them that "they contain absolutely nothing which one could not find more easily in Aesop, or in even more trivial books." As far as the Protestant Church went, the position in the Bible that Luther gave to the Apocrypha became the standard position. When printed in the Protestant English Bible they regularly come between the Old and the New Testaments in a section of their own.

The first complete English Bible was that of Coverdale in 1535, and Coverdale followed Luther's example with certain slight differences. Coverdale printed a translation of 1 and 2 Esdras; he did not print the Prayer of Manasseh; and in his first edition he printed Baruch after Jeremiah. In the 1537 edition Baruch too was placed in the appendix with the rest of the Apocrypha; and the fashion was set. Coverdale's introduction to the Apocrypha is interesting:

These books (good reader) which be called Apocrypha are not judged among the doctors to be of like reputation with the other scriptures. . . . And the chief cause thereof is this: there be many places in them that seem to be repugnant unto the open and manifest truth in the other books of the Bible. Nevertheless I have not gathered them together to the intent that I would have them despised, or little set by, or that I should think them false, for I am not able to prove it. Yea I doubt not verily, if they were equally conferred with the other open scripture (time, place and circumstance in all things considered) they would neither seem contrary, nor be untruly and perversely alleged. Truth it is: a man's face cannot be seen so well in a water as in a fair glass: neither can it be shewed so clearly in a water that is stirred or moved as in a still water. These and many other dark places of scripture have been sore stirred and mixed with blind and covetous opinions of men, which have cast such a mist before the eyes of the simple, that as long as they be not conferred with the other places of scripture, they shall not seem otherwise to be understood than as covetousness expoundeth them. But whosoever thou be that readest scripture, let the Holy Ghost be thy teacher, and let one text expound another unto thee. As for such dreams, visions and dark sentences as be hid from thy understanding, commit them unto God, and make no articles of them (i.e. base no doctrines on them). But let the plain text be thy guide, and the Spirit of God (which is the author thereof) shall lead thee in all truth.

Coverdale is, in effect, admitting the secondary character of the Apocrypha, and at the same time insisting that, properly used, they have their place and value.

The next date of note in the history of the Apocrypha in the English Bible is in the Bible of Thomas Matthew issued in 1537. It followed the custom of putting the Apocrypha by themselves between the Testaments, and it is notable in that it is the first English Bible to have in it the Prayer of Manasseh. Its version of the Prayer of Manasseh was translated from a French Version, from Olivetan's Bible.

The next pronouncement regarding the Apocrypha was in the Geneva Bible. This Bible was made in Geneva by a band of English reformers who had fled from England when the persecution under Queen Mary threatened. Their leader was William Whittingham who was married to a sister of John Calvin. This is one of the most famous of all English Bibles, and not even the Authorized Version succeeded at first in displacing it. Between 1560, when it first appeared, and 1630 no fewer than about two hundred editions of the Geneva Bible, either as a whole or of the New Testament separately, appeared. It was the Bible of Shakespeare and of John Bunyan and of Cromwell's army and of the Pilgrim Fathers. The Geneva Bible was one of the great English Bibles. It had the Apocrypha in the now normal place between the Testaments, with one very odd exception. It placed the Prayer of Manasseh between 2 Chronicles and Ezra. In the table of contents it appears as "The Prayer of Manasseh, apocryphe." And a note in the margin of the prayer itself says: "This prayer is not in the Ebrewe, but is translated out of the Greke." Why the Prayer of Manasseh received different treatment from the other books of the Apocrypha is unknown. The Geneva Bible also makes its own pronouncement about the Apocrypha in general:

These books that follow in order after the Prophets unto the New Testament are called Apocrypha; that is, books which were not received by a common consent to be read and expounded publically in the Church, neither yet served to prove any point of Christian religion, save inasmuch as they had the consent of the other Scriptures called canonical to confirm the same, or rather whereon they were grounded: but as books proceeding from godly men were received to be read for the advancement and furtherance of the knowledge of the history, and for the instruction of godly manners: which books declare that at all times God had an especial care for his Church and left them not utterly destitute of teachers and means to confirm them in the hope of the promised Messiah, and also witness that those calamities that God sent to his Church were according to his providence, who had both so threatened by his Prophets, and so brought it to pass for the destruction of their enemies, and for the trial of his children.

Like their predecessors, the translators of the Geneva Bible saw the books of the Apocrypha as valuable, but valuable only within their limits.

In the Authorized Version the Apocrypha stand between the Testaments without note or comment. The assumption is that this is their place, and no comment is needed. But Bruce Metzger points out one interesting fact about the Authorized Version and the Apocrypha. The Authorized Version had its marginal references, and they were relatively few, and in the Old Testament there were 102 references to the Apocrypha in the margin, and in the New Testament 11. In the Authorized Version the Apocrypha are still an integral part of the whole.

It seemed that the books of the Apocrypha had established themselves as a kind of appendix to the Old Testament, and that they had acquired the status of honorable though not fully inspired books. But soon the situation was to change. Men's attitude to the Apocrypha became a thing of strong feelings.

There was opposition from Protestants on the ground that the Roman Catholic Church were the real possessors of the Apocrypha. It was possible by means of the Apocrypha to justify things which were abhorrent to Protestant belief. The Reformers would have nothing to do with them, if they could be cited to lend support to doctrines which to them were anathema. And on general grounds the Puritans were highly suspicious of documents, purporting to be sacred and inspired, which were extra to Scripture.

However, it is interesting to note an experience which Bunyan relates in his autobiography *Grace abounding to the chief of Sinners.* About the year 1652 Bunyan went through a time of deep spiritual despondency. "One day," he said, "after I had been so many weeks oppressed and cast down, as I was now quite giving up the Ghost of all my hopes of ever attaining life, that sentence fell with weight upon my spirit, *Look at the generations of old and see: Did ever any trust in the Lord and was confounded?* At which I was greatly lightened and encouraged in my Soul; for thus at that very instant it was expounded to me: *Begin at the beginning of* Genesis, *and read to the end of the* Revelations, *and see if you can find that there was any that ever trusted in the Lord and was confounded.* So coming home I presently went to the Bible, to see if I could find that saying, not doubting but to find it presently; for it was so fresh, and with such strength and comfort on my spirit that I was as it talked with me." He goes on: "Well, I looked but I found it not. (This was in the days before concordances.) Only it abode upon me. . . . Thus I continued above a year, and could not find the place; but at last casting my eye into the *Apocrypha* books I found it in *Ecclesiasticus* (2:10)."

So, Bunyan almost apologizes for finding anything helpful in the Apocrypha! He goes on: "This, at the first, did somewhat daunt me; but because by this time I had got more experience of the love and kindness of God, it troubled me the less; especially when I considered that though it was not in those texts that we call Holy and Canonical, yet forasmuch as this sentence was the sum and substance of many of the Promises, it was my duty to take the comfort of it; and I bless God for that word, for it was God to me." "That word," he says, "doth still at times shine before my face." It is a most significant story, the story of a man who was almost afraid to be helped by the Apocrypha.

So at least in some quarters the tide was running against the Apocrypha, and the printers began to print the Bible without them. We can see that this began as a printer's doing for often we find the Apocrypha on the index page, and we find the pages which should have been there with the Apocrypha missing, with a blank in the page numbering between the Old and the New Testaments. It became difficult to buy a Bible with the Apocrypha.

The trend is now different. The last sentence of the Introduction to the Apocrypha in the Revised Standard Version is a quotation of a sentence from Frank C. Porter: "Modern historical interest . . . is putting the Apocrypha in their true place as significant documents of a most important era in religious history." And the New English Bible includes an excellent modern translation of these books.

Finally, we must ask, what then are we as Bible readers to say about the Apocrypha? In his book *What Books Belong in the Bible?* F. V. Filson puts the case strongly and convincingly for holding that the Apocrypha are not part of Scripture. He puts forward a series of arguments to prove his point of view.

1. He is quite sure that they were never meant to be regarded as Scripture. At no time was there ever a canon of the Septuagint, the Greek Old Testament, as there was of the Hebrew Old Testament. The number of extra books in the Septuagint was never laid down, and often varied. The extra books were never at any time given an official position as the books of the Hebrew Old Testament were. They are never at any time quoted by Jesus. They are never cited in the sermons of the early church, for instance, in the sermons recorded in Acts. No one in the apostolic age ever quoted them as Scripture. The plain fact is that wherever Hebrew was known, it was the Hebrew Old Testament which was regarded as Scripture. In the early church no one ever stated or even suggested that certain extra books had been added to the Old Testament. The place of these books in the church was due only to use and practice. They were used, but they were never regarded as authoritative in the sense that the Hebrew books were so held to be.

2. At no period in the history of the church, even in the later days, were they ever unanimously and unquestioningly accepted, not even as we have seen in the Roman Catholic Church. There was always a doubt about them and a question mark against them. And books whose place has always been controversial cannot be part of the Scripture of the church.

3. They have nothing to add to the religious thought and belief of the church. There is nothing in them that is not contained, and contained better, in the Old Testament. They have nothing to add to the books which were and are universally accepted.

4. In the case of the books of the Old Testament, their inspiration is self-evidencing, but in the case of the books of the Apocrypha, this is not so. As Filson puts it, "We accept the Old Testament as Scripture by a personal and group confession that these writings, when brought home by the Holy Spirit, speak God's indispensable word to us with effective power." And it is precisely this that the Apocrypha do not do. The surest way to see the secondary character of the Apocrypha is simply to read them. To do so is to experience the difference between them and the books which are unquestionably Scripture.

Dr. Filson will not even allow to these books a compromise position. "They are not Scripture," he says, "and they have no inherent right to a compromise position which practically treats them as Scripture while maintaining the fiction that they are without influence on doctrinal thinking."

But even if we hold that the apocryphal books have no claim to be regarded as Scripture, this is far from saying that we ought to, or can, completely discard them. They have an importance and a place.

1. To begin with, they have a place in literature. They contain some of the world's great stories, and they are part of the literature of the world with which every properly educated man should be familiar. The Apocrypha have had their influence on literature and on music and on art.

In his chapter on "The Pervasive Influence of the Apocrypha" in the *Introduction to the Apocrypha* Bruce Metzger outlines this influence in many spheres, and quotes one surprising example of it. It was certain things said in the Apocrypha which sent Columbus out to discover America! A famous fifteenth-century writer called Pierre d'Ailly, who was a great scholar and Archbishop of Cambrai, wrote a book entitled *Ymago Mundi,* the *Image of the World.* In it there is a chapter *De Quantitate terrae habitabilis,* Concerning the Amount of Earth which is Habitable. On the basis of 2 Esdras (4 Ezra) 6:42, 47, 50, 52 he argued that six-sevenths of the earth is land and only one seventh sea. The first passage reads: "On the third day thou didst command the waters to be gathered together in the seventh part of the earth; six parts thou didst dry up and keep so that some of them might be planted and cultivated and be of service before thee." This made d'Ailly argue that since the earth is a sphere, and since only one seventh is sea, the ocean between the west coast of Europe and the east coast of Asia can be "of no great width," and with a fair wind could be navigated in a few days. This is exactly what Columbus set out to prove. There was a copy of d'Ailly's book in Columbus' library, annotated in Columbus' own hand. It was this that sent Columbus voyaging, and it was this that at last persuaded hesitant sovereigns to finance his expedition, for here was a sacred book which said that the sea covered no more than one seventh of the earth, and could therefore easily be navigated!

2. The Apocrypha have a place in the moral literature of the

world. The moral advice given in Wisdom and Ecclesiasticus will never be out of date.

3. The Apocrypha contain indispensable historical material, as for instance, the story of the struggle of the Maccabees for the freedom of the Jews.

4. But the supreme use of the Apocrypha is that they bridge the gap between the Old and the New Testaments. In that gap there are three hundred years of which we will otherwise know very little. To move from the Old Testament to the New Testament is like jumping at one leap from the sixteenth to the nineteenth century. The great use of the Apocrypha is that they give us the political, cultural, ethical, and religious background of the contemporaries of Jesus Christ, and therefore help us better to understand the New Testament.

The importance of the Apocrypha cannot be doubted, and no student of the Bible can afford to disregard them.

Chapter 5
How to Study the Bible

All through this chapter I am going to assume that the person who wants to engage in the study of the Bible is a Christian, or at least wishes to be a Christian. We are to be thinking all the time of the person whose desire it is to widen his knowledge and to deepen and enrich his Christian life and experience by the study of the Bible. We begin with the assumption of Arminius that, "The Church is that community which recognizes the word of God in the Scriptures."

The Bible, of course, must be studied as any other book is studied. To it we must bring all the rigor and the apparatus of scholarship. It must be approached with all the willingness to make an effort with which the student approaches the study of any of the world's great books.

But there is another side of this question which is no less important. If it is true that the Bible is to be studied with the *methods* with which any great book is studied, it is equally true that the Bible is not studied for the *purpose* for which any other book is studied. An ordinary book is studied for information, for instruction, for interest, for pleasure, as a textbook, as a task; but the Bible is written that in it the reader may find life and encounter God. In about A.D. 1000 Aelfric, one of the very early translators of the Bible, wrote a noble passage on what he felt the Bible to be.

Whoever would be one with God must often and often read the Holy Scriptures. For when we pray we speak to God; and, when we read the Bible, God speaks to us. The reading of the Scriptures produces a twofold advantage to the reader. It renders him wiser by informing his mind; and also leads him from the vanities of the world to the love of God. The reading of the Scriptures is truly an honorable employment, and greatly conduces to the purity of the soul. For as the body is nourished by natural food, so the sublimer man, that is, the soul, is nourished by the divine saying, according to the words of the Psalmist: "How sweet are thy words unto my taste, yea, sweeter than honey to my mouth." Happy is he, then, who reads the Scriptures if he convert the words into actions. The whole of the Scriptures are written for our salvation, and by them we obtain the knowledge of the

truth. The blind man stumbles oftener than he who sees; so he w
ignorant of the precepts of Scripture offends more frequently tr.
he who knows them.

1. So then, in the very first place, the reader must bring reverence to the Bible. His duty will be to begin his reading with prayer. Luther said of the student of Scripture that his "first duty is to begin with a prayer of such a nature that God in his great mercy may grant you the true understanding of his words." The Psalmist prayed: "Open my eyes that I may behold wondrous things out of thy law" (Psalm 119:18), and we may well use the prayer that many of us know and love:

> Blessed Lord, who hast caused all holy Scriptures to be written for our learning, grant that we may in such wise hear them, read, mark, learn, and inwardly digest them, that by patience and comfort of thy holy word, we may embrace and ever hold fast the blessed hope of everlasting life, which thou hast given us in our Savior Jesus Christ.

We will do well to take our thoughts back to the Jewish idea of the Spirit. As the Jew saw it, the Spirit of God does two things. First, the Spirit brings God's truth to men. Second, and just as important, the Spirit enables men to recognize God's truth when they see it. This is to say that the same Spirit who moved the writers of the Bible to write their books is the Spirit who now enables us to study and to interpret these books.

We may see how the Spirit came to open the Bible to one of the greatest Christians of all time. Writing in 1545 Luther tells us how in his younger days he hated the very word *righteousness.* To him it always brought the idea that God in his righteousness is out to punish the unrighteous and the sinner. It was to him a word of terror. He never could understand the connection of the two halves of Romans 1:17: "For therein is the righteousness of God revealed from faith to faith: as it is written, The just shall live by faith." For days and nights he thought and meditated upon this text; and then he began to see that the word *righteousness* means that God in his mercy justifies man by faith. To put it very simply, he began to see that the righteousness of God is not the righteousness with which he threatens us, but *the righteousness which he offers us and gives us.* Then he writes:

> At this point I felt completely reborn, and as if I had entered paradise with its open gate. In a moment the whole meaning of Scripture

...med to have changed. Thereafter I ran through the Scriptures as
. I had them in my memory, and collected analogical meanings in
other words, such as the work of God, which means the work that God
works in *us*, the virtue of God, which means the virtue through which
he makes *us* powerful, the wisdom of God, which means the wisdom
through which he makes *us* wise, the courage of God, the salvation of
God, the glory of God. My love for that sweetest word *righteousness of
God* was henceforth as great as my hatred for it had been hitherto. In
this way this passage of Paul was truly the gate of Paradise.

In one blinding flash of illumination the meaning of the passage
had blazed upon him, and the meaning was not the way to
knowledge but the way to paradise, when he saw that anything
that is *of* God is *for* the man who has faith. To study Scripture
with reverence is the way to illumination by the continued
action of the Spirit of God.

Let us take another example. Luther and Erasmus were two
of the great figures of the Reformation, but they were very
different. Erasmus was the grammarian, the philologist. He
would identify the meaning of a word, disentangle the
grammar of a passage—none could do so better—but there he
left it. With theological definition he refused to become
entangled. But Luther began where Erasmus left off. He asked,
not only, What does this mean? but also, What does this mean
for me? Erasmus had defined the meaning of *penitence*—it is "a
change of mind and the understanding of one's own sin, after
having suffered harm, and having recognized the mistake."
There he left it, and there Luther took it up. Luther said—and
said rightly—that such a change and such a recognition cannot
take place "without a change of sentiment and love." A man's
affections have to be set on different things, before he sees the
error of the old things. Then Luther went on to say
further—and rightly—such a change of sentiment and love can
only be effected by the grace of God. A man cannot change
himself—grace has to do that. So then Luther took the third
step and declared that penitence is "a transmutation of mind
and sentiment effected by grace"—and that, he said, is the
translation of *metanoia,* penitence.

Here we have the difference. Erasmus approached the word
penitence in the spirit of the man who would make a definition
of it to grace a dictionary; Luther approached it in the spirit of
the man who wanted to find salvation for his own soul, and for
the souls of men. The grammarian and the theologian, the

philologist and the evangelist—both are needed. But the really Christian study of Scripture approaches it in the attitude of that reverence which is seeking more than grammatical accuracy; it is seeking and finding the grace of God.

2. The second rule for the study of Scripture is that it is best done within the fellowship of the church. This does not mean ruling out Bible study on one's own. But the Second Letter of Peter lays it down: "First of all you must understand this, that no prophecy of Scripture is a matter of one's own interpretation" (2 Peter 1:20). To Study Scripture wisely we must study it within the tradition of the church.

To take the matter at its simplest this is the only sensible thing to do. If a man begins to study medicine, he does not start as if no one had never studied medicine before. He enters into the discoveries and the works and the wisdom of all who went before. If a man embarks on the study of any branch of science, the first thing he does is to study the work that has been done on that part of the subject up until now. It would be a matter of folly—and arrogant folly at that—if when we came to the study of any passage of Scripture we completely neglected all that the scholarship and the devotion of the past had learned about it. It is an obvious fact that all learning begins in a fellowship of learning, and Christian learning should begin in the Christian church. Luther said that the study of Scripture is only possible for a Christian. He held, and he held rightly, that to study any work profitably the experience of the reader must at least to some extent correspond with the experience of the writer. He held that it was a condition of any understanding of Scripture that the person who studies it must have a knowledge of Christ, since he, "the sun and truth in Scripture," is spoken of everywhere in the Bible, in the Old Testament as in the New. "The deeper the understanding of Christ," as Schwartz puts it in *Biblical Translation,* "the deeper the understanding of Scripture." The Christian studies Scripture both because he knows Christ and wants to know Christ.

Luther always held that Jerome's Latin Bible, the Vulgate, was not a good translation, because Jerome had produced it alone, and had thereby lost the promise that, where two or three are gathered together in his name, Jesus Christ is with them (Matthew 18:20). The study of the Bible in a Christian fellowship is richer than the study of the Bible in isolation and alone.

We have here three principles. First, no man can find the truth alone. Second, no human endeavor is effective without the Spirit and the grace of God. Third, no conclusion is valid, if it is arrived at having no regard for the fellowship of the church.

3. The student of the Bible must study the Bible honestly. This is to say, he must go to the Bible to find out and to seek the truth, and not to prove a case about which he has already made up his mind. It is common—it is almost usual—for people to use the Bible as an arsenal of proof texts to prove things about which they have already made up their minds. A man can use the Bible to find in it what he wants to find. He can use it to hear the echo of his own voice rather than the sound of the voice of God. Tyndale once said that the students who were taught by the priests and the monks came to the Bible "armed with false principles, with which they are clean shut out of the understanding of Scripture." Arminius once said: "Nothing is more obstructive to the investigation of the truth than prior commitments to partial truths." This is simply to say that not even God can teach a man who comes to the Bible with his mind made up.

F. C. Grant in *How to Read the Bible* tells how an ancient rabbi once satirized his rival by saying: "When Rabbi Eliezer expounds, he begins by saying, 'Scripture, be silent, while I am interpreting.' " Hugh Pope in *English Versions of the Bible* quotes Gardiner as saying: "Scripture is a sweet, pure flower, whereof spiders gather poison and bees honey. . . . Go thither instructed with wholesome doctrine and thou shalt see it confirmed. Go thither infected with malicious opinions and then thou shalt writhe out matter wherewith to maintain them." When we study the Bible we should be very sure that we are listening for God and not for the echo of our own voice.

4. If we are going to make the honest approach to Scripture, it specially means one thing. It means that our approach must be to *the whole of Scripture*. It is possible by making a selective approach to Scripture to argue in precisely opposite directions. If we quote Ecclesiastes 9:10: "Whatever your hand finds to do, do it with your might; for there is no work or thought or knowledge or wisdom in Sheol, to which you are going," we can argue that there is no life after death. If we quote 1 Corinthians 15:19: "If for this life only we have hoped in Christ, we are of all men most to be pitied," we can argue that to remove the belief in a life after death is to cut the vital nerve of the Christian faith. If

we quote the Old Testament law of an eye for an eye and a tooth for a tooth (Exodus 21:24; Leviticus 24:20; Deuteronomy 19:21) we can argue for the punishment of criminals by force, and, for instance, for the death penalty. If on the other hand we quote the command of Jesus to turn the other cheek and to love our enemies (Matthew 5:39, 44), then we can argue that purely retributory and vindictive punishment has no place in Christian society. If we quote Matthew 25:46: "And they will go away into eternal punishment, but the righteous into eternal life," we can argue that after death some go to eternal bliss and some to eternal hell by the judgment of God. If we quote John 12:32: "I, when I am lifted up from the earth, will draw all men to myself," we can argue for universal salvation.

There is nothing which so bedevils theological discussion as the one-sided and selective approach to Scripture, the approach in which a man quotes and cites that which suits his own point of view and agrees with his own case, and at the same time deliberately ignores all the material on the other side. That is why argument and discussion based on the quotation of texts can never get anywhere.

When we study Scripture we have to take the whole of Scripture to our problem and to our thought. We have to look at the matter, not in the light of any text or series of texts, but in the light of the whole mind and character of Jesus Christ as we know them, and in the light of the mind and heart of that God, who is the God and Father of our Lord Jesus Christ. An honest approach to the Bible is an approach to the whole Bible, and not a selection from the Bible to suit ourselves.

5. Still further, and equally important, we have to take the whole of ourselves to the study of Scripture. Jesus said that we must love God with all our heart and soul and strength and mind (Luke 10:27), and that is the way in which we have to study the Bible.

There always have been some people who consciously or unconsciously left their minds behind them when they began to study Scripture. F. C. Grant in his book *How to Read the Bible* tells of an experience of a friend of his. His friend had been talking of how to study the Old Testament, and of how there are times when the Old Testament can be a difficult book. At the end of the talk a bright attractive young woman rose and said: "You don't need someone to tell you how to read the Bible. Open it anywhere, read three verses, make your mind a blank, then the

Holy Spirit will do the rest!" The one thing you did not need, as she saw it, was intelligence; the one thing you did not use was your mind.

So then there is with some this suspicion of human reason, "the devil's whore," as Luther called it. But Luther was like so many great preachers who are men of passion and enthusiasm and conviction. He was very apt to stress one side of a question at a time, and it is often quite unsafe to regard anything he says as his final view of any subject, until you have checked up on the other side. Luther can argue—and argue rightly—that more than intellect is needed for the study of the Bible. He can and does argue that human and celestial wisdom are not the same thing. He can and does argue that it is not in human power, it is not in the scope of the human intellect, to understand the word of God. He can say, "Offer your empty heart to God, and the truth will be revealed."

Luther can certainly argue that the human intellect is quite inadequate to understand the word of God; he can certainly argue that a man's intellect may be his biggest handicap. "Reason is the devil's whore, and can do nothing but shame and disgrace everything that God does." "Faith strikes dead this reason, and kills this beast, which heaven and earth and all creatures cannot destroy." "Reason cannot rightly accord to God his deity nor attribute it to him as his own, though it rightly belongs to him alone. It knows that God exists. But who or what person it may be who is properly called God it does not know. . . . Thus reason plays blind man's buff with God, and makes vain errors, and always misses the mark, calling God what is not God, and not calling God what is God." No one has ever spoken more contemptuously about human reason than Martin Luther.

But there is another side to this, and, when it is stated by Luther, the matter is perfectly reasonable. True, Scripture is given by the Spirit and can be understood only by the Spirit. It is only the author of Scripture who can interpret Scripture. "But the message of the Spirit is transmitted through language." "Words are the vehicles of thought; they are like the shrine in which God's truth is found." And there is need of the hardest kind of thought, the most intense kind of study, the most strenuous bringing to bear of the reason on the subject, to find the meaning of the words. This is where reason comes in. Reason has to be brought to bear on the givenness of the message of the Spirit. Devotion will grasp the message of the Spirit through grace; scholarship will toil at the meaning of the words in which the message is expressed.

So Melanchthon writes in the *Encomium Eloquentiae (In Praise of Eloquence):* "I have not the mistaken view that the holy can be penetrated through the industry of human talent. There is something in the holy that no one can ever see, unless it is shown to him by God: and Christ cannot be known to use without the Holy Spirit teaching us. . . . But apart from prophecy, the meaning of words must be known, in which, as in a shrine, the divine mysteries are hidden. For what is the use of reciting in a magic way words that have not been understood? Is it not like telling a story to a deaf person?" The mind of man has to toil to understand and to communicate the message of the Spirit. Luther himself said that the Scripture teaches eternal life, and for that very reason it cannot be understood without the Spirit. Therefore a man must pray to receive illumination, guidance and understanding. "But God will grant understanding only to him who perseveres in the study of words themselves, and meditates upon the meaning with which they are informed by that Holy Spirit."

The interaction between the Spirit of God and the mind of man is established. The Spirit helps the man who toils to help himself. God does not spoonfeed a man. The more a man brings to the Bible, the more he gets from it. When the grace and guidance of the Spirit meet the study, the toil and the endeavor of a dedicated mind, then indeed Scripture opens its riches. A man has to bring the whole of himself—heart and mind—to the whole of Scripture.

6. One last general point concerning our attitude to Scripture must be noted before we turn to detail. The study of Scripture is meant to lead to action. We often hear of a *discussion* circle, but if the work of a circle ends in discussion there is something far wrong; it must end in action. J. A. Bengel had on his New Testament the famous two lines:

Te totum applica ad textum;
Rem totam applica ad te.

This we may paraphrase: "Apply the whole of yourself to the study of Scripture; and then apply the whole of the result of your study to yourself."

...d as Luther noted, in the last analysis it is not the ...ulations of a book with which we are dealing; it is the ...mmands of a person, Jesus Christ. As Luther wrote in a letter ...o John Staupitz: "For thus do the commands of God become sweet, when we understand that they are not to be read in books only, but in the wounds of the sweetest Savior."

When we study the word of God in a group, we should not do so for the sake of a pleasant argument and discussion; we should do so to find for ourselves the will of God, and having found it, we should not only know, we should also obey.

We have spoken about the attitude of study. Let us now come to the actual technique of our study. We begin with one thing which must be clear. Our aim from beginning to end must be to find out what the Bible means. That sounds comparatively easy, but it is just here that the task of study has so often been complicated and wrongly conceived.

The ancient Jewish scholars used to say that Scripture has four meanings. First, there is *Peshat,* the simple literal meaning. Second, there is *Remez,* the meaning by allusion, the meaning which the student can arrive at when he treats a passage not just as a straightforward narrative but as an allegory. Third, there is *Derash,* which means the homiletic application of the passage after it has been studied with all the aids to study available. And fourth there is *Sod,* which is the inner meaning, the meaning to which only the spiritual expert can penetrate. *P*eshat, *R*emez, *D*erash, *S*od—note the initial letters of the words—P R D S. Hebrew has no vowels, only consonants; the vowels have to specially inserted, and PRDS are the consonants of the Hebrew word for Paradise, and so the ancient scholars claimed that, if a student penetrated fully into these four meanings, he would be here and now in Paradise! But where they went wrong was that they neglected the simple, literal meaning, and went all out for the allegorical and the inner meanings, and once we start allegorizing Scripture we can make it mean anything.

Here is a comparatively simple example of how they allegorized. The passage is Ecclesiastes 9:14, 15:

> There was a little city with few men in it; and a great king came against it and besieged it, building great siegeworks against it. But there was found in it a poor wise man, and he by his wisdom delivered the city. Yet no one remembered that poor man.

That is a simple parable of the way in which people forget has been done for them and are guilty of ingratitude. Now of the basic beliefs of the Jews about human nature is that every man there are two natures, the good nature and the bad nature; the good nature urges the man to goodness, and the evil nature tries to seduce him into sin. So the rabbis allegorized this parable. "There was a little city"—that is, the body. "With few men in it"—the few men are the limbs of the body. "A great king came against it"—that is the evil nature, the evil impulse. "Building great siegeworks against it"—the great siegeworks are the sins. "But there was found in it a poor wise man"—that is, the good nature, the good impulse. "He by his wisdom delivered the city"—this means repentance and good works by which a man is saved. "Yet no one remembered that poor man"—because at the time the evil impulse holds sway the good impulse is altogether forgotten. Thus a simple story of ingratitude is turned into a complicated allegory of human nature.

Christian scholars for many centuries did exactly the same. The scholars of the Middle Ages had four Latin lines which spoke of the fourfold meaning of Scripture:

> *Litera gesta docet;*
> *Quid credas, allegoria;*
> *Moralis, quid agat;*
> *Quid speres, anagogia.*

The translation is:

> The literal tells what happened;
> The allegorical, what you are to believe;
> The moral, what you are to do;
> The anagogical, what you may hope for.

Schwartz *(Biblical Translation,* p. 47) fills it out: "The literal sense explains the historical contents, the allegorical elucidates matters of faith by revealing the allegory contained in the biblical text, the moral sense indicates rules of human conduct, the anagogical sense deals with the future you may hope for (in the life to come)."

The trouble in the Christian approach to the Bible has often tended to be the way in which inner meanings were always being looked for in Scripture, and in which simple stories were given

al meanings. The Greeks did this with Homer long
re the Jews began doing it with the Old Testament. Take a
ek example. The Greeks had a god named Hermes. They
en went on to derive *Hermes* from the Greek verb *erein,* which
means *to speak.* Next they went on to say that Hermes is not
meant to be taken as a person at all; he is a symbol, an allegory of
the power of speech. They then went on to explain on these
lines the various ways in which Hermes is described. He is called
the *conductor,* because speech *conducts* one man's thoughts into
his neighbor's soul. He is represented with *winged* feet, which
stand for *winged words.* He is called *the leader of souls* because
words soothe the soul to rest. He is called *the awakener from sleep,*
because words rouse men to action. He carries a staff with
serpents twined round it, and the serpents stand for the savage
natures which are calmed by words (Edwin Hatch, *The Influence
of Greek Ideas and Usages upon the Christian Church,* p. 63). So the
god Hermes is allegorized into the power of speech.

The Jews did this regularly. Sarah and Hagar are the symbols
of true wisdom and pagan philosophy. Lot's wife symbolizes the
attachment of the soul to earthly things, an attachment which
produces blindness to God and to his truth.

It is obvious that, if you treat Scripture like this, you can make
it mean almost anything you choose. The most notorious
example of this is Augustine's interpretation of the Parable of
the Good Samaritan, which C. H. Dodd quotes in his book on
the *Parables of the Kingdom.*

A certain man went down from Jerusalem to Jericho—Adam is meant;
Jerusalem is the heavenly city of peace from the blessedness of which
Adam fell; *Jericho* means the moon, and signifies our mortality,
because it is born, waxes, wanes and dies. *Thieves* are the devil and his
angels. *Who stripped him*—that is, of his immortality; *and left him half
dead*—because insofar as a man can understand and know God, he
lives, but insofar as he is wasted and oppressed by sin, he is dead; he is
therefore called *half dead.* The *Priest* and the *Levite* who saw him and
passed by signify the priesthood and ministry of the Old Testament,
which could profit nothing for salvation, *Samaritan* came from a
Hebrew derivation meaning *guardian,* and therefore the Lord
himself is signified by this name. *The binding of the wounds* is the
restraint of sin. *Oil* is the comfort of a good hope, *wine* is the
exhortation to work with a fervent spirit. The *beast* is the flesh in
which Jesus came to us. The being *set upon the beast* is belief in the
incarnation of Christ. The *inn* is the Church, where travellers are
refreshed on their return from pilgrimage to their heavenly country.

The *morrow* is after the Resurrection of the Lord. The *two pe*
either the two precepts of love, or, possibly, the two sacraments.
innkeeper is the apostle Paul. *The promise he makes to pay any extra expe*
incurred is either his counsel of celibacy, or the fact that he worke
with his hands lest he be a burden to the brethren.

If this is what the parable really means, it is obvious that no
ordinary person could ever be expected to discover its meaning
for himself; and it is also obvious that there is no limit to the
number of meanings that a man could find in any passage of
Scripture.

There is another famous instance of what allegorization can
do in the Letter of Barnabas 9:7-9. Barnabas starts out from
Genesis 17:23, 27. We there learn of the beginning of
circumcision and that Abraham circumcised all the males in his
household. By adding Genesis 14:14 to this we find that the
number of them can be reckoned as *three hundred and eighteen.* In
the Greek of the Septuagint, from which Barnabas is working,
the number comes in the order *eighteen men and three hundred.*
Now Greek has no figures for the numerals; the numerals are
represented by letters of the alphabet, as if in English A were to
equal 1, B were to equal 2, and so on. Well then, the Greek for
eighteen is the letter *iota,* I, which stands for 10, and *eta,* the long
Greek E, which stands for 8. That is to say, 18 is IE, which as
anyone can see is the first two letters of the name IESOUS,
which is Jesus. The Greek for *three hundred,* is the letter *tau,* T,
and T is the shape of the Roman cross on which Jesus was
crucified. So Barnabas says that *three hundred and eighteen* is IE,
which stands for Jesus, and T which stands for the cross, and
therefore when Abraham performed the first act of circumcision he did so "looking forward to the spirit of Jesus."

This is a fatal way of interpreting Scripture. It is a method
which we should entirely avoid. The meaning for which we look
is the meaning which the writer originally meant, not the
meaning which later ingenuity can read into the text. To this
day preachers often use allegorizations, not, it is true, with the
perverted ingenuity with which the ancient interpreters used it,
but in a more restrained way. That very great preacher James S.
Stewart in his book of sermons *The Gates of New Life* has a
sermon on Acts 27:29: "Then fearing lest we should have fallen
upon rocks, they cast four anchors out of the stern, and wished
for the day." He calls the sermon "Anchors of the Soul." He
goes on to say that every soul should have four anchors—the

...s of hope, duty, prayer, and the cross of Christ. A simple
...n of sailors in the middle of a storm has been turned into an
...gorization of the supports of the soul in the storms of life.
he use of this method by even so great a preacher cannot
justify it for us. It is the original meaning of Scripture that we
must set out to find.

If our primary task is to find out the meaning of Scripture,
then the beginning of our study must be the study of words. We
take only two illustrations of how illuminating the study of
words can be.

Three times Paul speaks about the *earnest of the Spirit.* The
word for earnest is *arrabôn. Arrabôn* is a word from business and
commercial Greek. An *arrabôn* was the part of a purchase price
or a contract price, paid in advance, as a guarantee that the full
price would in due time be paid. So a woman sells a cow, and
gets so much as *arrabôn* in guarantee that the full price will be
paid. A man engages a mousecatcher. Mice did a great deal of
harm in the vineyards at harvest time, and he pays him so much
as *arrabôn,* so that he will begin on the extermination of the pests
straight away. A group of castanet dancing-girls are engaged
for a village festivity, and they are at once paid so much as
arrabôn, as a guarantee that the full contract price will be paid
after they have performed. An *arrabôn* was a first installment of
the full purchase price, and a guarantee that the full purchase
price would be paid. So Paul speaks of the Holy Spirit as God's
arrabôn. This is to say that for the Christian the gift of the Spirit
is the first installment of the life of heaven, and the guarantee
that some day that heavenly life in all its fullness will come.

Very commonly the Holy Spirit is called the Comforter. In
the Authorized Version in John's Gospel, Comforter is the title
and description of the Holy Spirit (John 14:16, 26; 15:26; 16:7).
There are few things which have so limited and truncated the
real work of the Holy Spirit as the consistent use of this word
Comforter. The word in Greek is *Paraklêtos,* which is sometimes
transliterated into English in the form *Paraclete,* as in the hymn,
"Come, thou holy Paraclete."

The Greek word *paraklêtos* literally means *someone who is called
in to the side of someone else.* In Greek the meaning of the word is
always decided by the purpose for which the person is called in.
It may mean someone called in to give evidence for the defense,
a witness in favor. It may mean someone called in to plead one's

cause, an advocate for the defense. It could mean so...
summoned to render medical aid, a physician. It is use...
describe someone speaking to the men of a depressed a...
dispirited army, who by his words and the impact of h...
personality puts fresh strength and courage into them.

It can be seen from these examples that a *paraklētos* is
someone who is called in to help one who is in difficulties to cope
with the situation. So then the Holy Spirit is the person through
whom there come to us the strength and grace of God to enable
us to cope with life. Certainly, part of this work is to comfort, but
only part. To call the Holy Spirit the Comforter, and to stop
there, is to have a limited and rather sentimental view of the
Spirit, whereas in the Greek the word is full of power and of the
promise of the God-given ability to face and to master any
situation in life.

How then did this word *Comforter* get into the English
translation of the Bible? It came in with Wycliffe about 1386,
and it has stayed ever since. But in the days of Wycliffe it was a
perfect translation. The word *comfort* is derived from the Latin
word *fortis,* which means *brave,* and originally the word meant
someone who puts courage into you. Let us take two other
examples of it in Wycliffe. Wycliffe translates Ephesians 6:10,
"Be ye *comforted* in the Lord." And he translates 1 Timothy
1:12, "I do thankings to him who *comforted* me." In both cases
the word in the Greek is *endunamoun,* whose root word is
dunamis, power, from which the word *dynamite* comes. In
Wycliffe's day to comfort a person was to fill that person with a
power like spiritual dynamite. The Holy Spirit does not simply
come and wipe our tears away; he gives us a dynamic power to
cope with life.

So then the first step in the technique of the study of the Bible
must be to ascertain the meaning of the passage which is being
studied, and that study must start with the investigation into the
meaning of words. This means that, ideally speaking, a Bible
study group should be led by someone who knows the original
languages Hebrew and Greek. This will be an obviously
impossible demand. Failing that, the group should have access
to someone who possesses such knowledge. But even that is an
impossible demand. The assumption would be that the minister
of the church would be such a person, but modern methods of
ministerial training do not necessarily include training in the
original languages. So the group will probably need to depend

... use of commentaries which have been made for English
...ers and which are in English, but which are founded on the
...iginal languages. Some such commentaries are listed at the
back of the book.

Our search for meaning will bring us to another necessity. If
we are to ascertain the meaning of any passage of Scripture, we
shall need to use a modern translation. The Authorized Version
is a version which will always be known and loved as one of the
supreme achievements of the English language, but there are at
least three reasons why, from the point of view of study, it is now
an inadequate translation.

1. There are passages in it which have now ceased to be
intelligible to modern ears, or in which the meaning of words
has altered. The astonishing thing in a translation made in 1611
is not that such things exist in it, but that on the whole there are
so few. Here are some examples of that.

They *fetched a compass* of seven days' journey. (2 Kings 3:9)

From thence *we fetched a compass* and came to Rhegium. (Acts 28:13)

To fetch a compass means to make a circuit.

There is in the AV a now-abandoned and often-misleading
use of the word *prevent*.

The sorrows of hell compassed me about; the snares of death
prevented me. (Psalm 18:5)

Why did the knees *prevent* me? or why the breasts that I should suck?
(Job 3:12)

In the morning shall my prayer *prevent* thee. (Psalm 88:13)

The inhabitants of the land of Tema brought water to him that was
thirsty, they *prevented* with their bread him that fled. (Isaiah 21:14)

In modern English the word *prevent* means to hinder, to
impede, to stop a person doing something; in the language of
1611 it meant to go before, to precede, and therefore to meet or
to encounter, but with no thought of hindrance, or prevention
in the modern sense of the term.

There is a still more misleading use of the word *conversation*.

Ye have heard of my *conversation* in time past in the Jews' religion.
(Galatians 1:13)

Be thou an example of the believers, in word, in *conversation,* in
charity, in spirit, in faith, in purity. (1 Timothy 4:12)

Who is a wise man and endued with knowledge among you? let
show out of a good *conversation* his works with meekness of wisα
(James 3:13)

Be ye holy in all manner of *conversation*. (1 Peter 1:15)

Having your *conversation* honest among the Gentiles. (1 Peter 2:12)

In modern language a man's *conversation* is the way in which he
talks; it is his speech, his language, his thought. But the word
conversation comes from the Latin *conversari,* which means to
walk up and down, to go to and fro, and it therefore means, not
his talk, but his whole conduct and behavior. In all these
instances we have quoted it is not a question of being careful of
our talk, but of being careful of our whole behavior, of our
whole life and conduct. The last instance is doubly deceiving. In
it *honest* does not mean telling the truth. In 1611 the word *honest*
far more commonly meant *honorable.* And so 1 Peter 2:12 really
means: "In your contact with the Gentile world see that your
conduct is always honorable."

It is quite clear that in our search for meaning we need a
translation which speaks the language not of the seventeenth
but of the twentieth century.

2. There is another characteristic of the Authorized Version
which it is relevant to note. The great characteristic of the
Authorized Version is the beauty of its English, and this beauty
is accompanied by a certain archaism. The language is
beautiful, but the language is not the language of the twentieth
century, and it is precisely this combination of beauty and
archaism which gives the Authorized Version the solemnity and
the dignity which are dear to so many. Now a translation should
reproduce not only the meaning of the original but also the
atmosphere of the original.

In the case of the Old Testament the atmosphere of the
Authorized Version is not at fault, for the Hebrew of the Old
Testament is for the most part classical Hebrew, Hebrew at its
best. But in the case of the New Testament the matter is very
different. The Greek of the New Testament is colloquial Greek;
it is the kind of Greek that people spoke on the street in the first
century. It is not classical Greek. We have noted that, even if the
New Testament were to lose all its religious importance, it
would still have a unique importance in that it is the only written
monument of that colloquial spoken Greek of the first century.
Now here is the point—the more solemn and dignified and

...ful and archaic a translation of the New Testament is, the ...se a translation it is. The New Testament in translation ...ould not sound beautiful and dignified and solemn and old; it ...hould sound modern, colloquial, the kind of language people speak in their homes and on the street, the kind of language they read in their newspapers. In the case of the New Testament a solemn, dignified, archaic translation could not be a worse translation, for that is all that the New Testament Greek is not.

Any translation of the New Testament ought to speak to a man in the vernacular in which he speaks; any other kind of translation is a bad translation.

So then in 1611 the Authorized Version was a good translation—but not now. When Luther spoke about his own translation of the Bible, he said that it was not to those who spoke Latin that the translator must go. "We must ask the mother in the home, the children on the street, the common man in the marketplace about this, and look them in the mouth to see how they speak, and afterward do our translating." The first essential of a New Testament for use in the study of its meaning is a New Testament in the language of our own generation.

3. The third fact about the Authorized Version is the most serious of all. It is obvious that no translation can be better than the manuscripts on which it is founded. Before printing was invented manuscripts were of course copied by hand. Even with the most careful copying by hand new errors crept in with each successive copying. Therefore, the older a manuscript is the more correct it is likely to be. The nearer it is to the original, the fewer removes there are between it and the author's original writing, the more accurate it will be. Further, the more manuscripts there are available, the more likely it is that in some of them the original readings will be preserved.

The Authorized Version was published in 1611. It was made from a Greek text, in the case of the New Testament, which was largely that of Erasmus, revised by Beza and Stephanus. This Greek text was based on not more than ten Greek manuscripts, of which the earliest was not earlier than the tenth century. This is to say, that the Authorized Version is a translation of a Greek text of the New Testament which is quite inadequate. This was not the fault of the translators; nor was it the fault of those who constructed the text which was used. They used the best that

was available in 1611. But since then all kinds of disco
have been made, and many new manuscripts have come to l₁
We have now available manuscripts which go back to the th₁.
and fourth centuries, and the manuscripts which are now
available can be numbered by the score, and even by the
hundred. This is to say that in the twentieth century there are
available manuscripts which are up to seven or eight hundred
years older than the manuscripts which were the basis of the
Greek text from which the Authorized Version was translated,
and there are hundreds more of them.

Much as we love the Authorized Version as a monument of
English prose, much as we rest our hearts in its music and in its
cadences, we cannot do anything other than recognize that in
the twentieth century it is no longer an adequate translation.
This is not to say that we are to stop reading the Authorized
Version for spiritual and devotional purposes; but it is to say
that it can no longer be properly used as the basis of real Bible
study. For the purposes of study we must use either the Revised
Standard Version, or, better still, the New English Bible. To
refuse to make the change is to shut our eyes deliberately to the
new knowledge of his word which God in our day and
generation has made available for us.

When we have established the meaning of the passage, so far
as the actual wording goes, the next task is to put the passage
into its context and into its background. It is impossible to
understand a person without understanding something about
his background. It is, for instance, impossible to understand
why a person is what he is, until we know something about his
home and his parents and how he was brought up. So it is
important to know *that* a thing happened; it is even more
important to know *why* it happened; and to know this it is
necessary to know the context and the background of the event.
Let us take two examples of this, one from the area of
geography and one from the area of life and customs.

One of the supreme differences between modern and ancient
times is the annihilation of distance. A man may nowadays
breakfast in London and lunch in New York over three
thousand miles away. The world today is a small place, and the
life people live today is a mobile life. Jesus, however, in his life in
Palestine was never as far as we know more than a hundred
miles from home. When we read the Samuel story in the first
two chapters of 1 Samuel it seems that Hannah and the boy

el are very far apart. Once a year she goes to see him and s with her the little coat that she had made for him. The urney has all the atmosphere of an expedition, and yet in fact Ramah, where Hannah lived, and Shiloh, where the child Samuel served, were about seventeen miles apart! Take the case of the Flood in Genesis 6. There the Flood is told of in terms of a world event. But for the writer of that story the world is Mesopotamia and the Euphrates Valley. America, Africa, Australia, Britain—the ancient writer had no conception that these continents and countries even existed. To him the world was that small part of it he knew. And that there was a flood in that area is one of the facts of history about which there is no doubt whatever. The flood devastated the only world the ancient writer knew, but we must not think that the word *world* meant to him a world in which three thousand miles is a morning's journey.

Take a more detailed example—Jesus' cleansing of the Temple. The cleansing of the Temple is one of the most terrifying stories in the Gospel history. The idea of the white hot anger of Jesus, the picture of the Jesus with the whip, are frightening conceptions. Let us then see first of all where this incident happened. It happened in the Court of the Gentiles. The Temple in Jerusalem was composed of a series of courts, and the entry into each court was increasingly limited. Into the Court of the Gentiles, anyone, Jew or Gentile might come. Next came the Court of the Women beyond which no woman could go. Between it and the Court of the Gentiles there was a low wall, into which there were inset stone tablets warning any Gentile that for him to proceed beyond this wall was a crime for which the penalty was instant death. Beyond the Court of the Women was the Court of the Israelites beyond which no layman could go. Finally there was the Court of the Priests in which were the great altar, and the seven-branched candlestick, and the table of the showbread, and the altar of the incense, and into it only the priests could go. At the far end of the Court of the Priests stood the Temple proper, the Holy Place and the Holy of Holies, into which only the High Priest could go, and he on the occasion of the Day of Atonement only. So then the farther into the Temple the various courts went, the fewer people were allowed into them. And this incident of the cleansing of the Temple happened in the one area of the Temple into which a

Gentile might come. If the Gentile was to worship and the Temple at all, here alone he might do so.

Next, who are the characters involved? First, there are money-changers. Every male Jew and proselyte—women an minors were exempt—had to pay a Temple tax of one half-shekel per year. A half-shekel was the equivalent of about fifteen cents. But this must be evaluated in light of the fact that a working man's daily wage averaged about eight cents. The tax was near enough two days' pay—which is quite something. Further, this Temple tax had to be paid in either sanctuary shekels or Galilean shekels. This was so because these were the only coins which had no king's head on them, and a coin with a king's head was for a Jew a graven image, especially since so many kings were given divine honor. For all ordinary purposes in Palestine any coinage would do and was valid—Greek, Roman, Phoenician, Egyptian, Syrian, and so on. The tax was paid at Passover time, and people came from all over the world to keep the Passover and to pay their tax. With them they brought all kinds of money. They were bound to pay. Within Palestine, if a man did not pay, the Temple authorities could and did distrain upon his goods. So the pilgrims went to the money-changers to have their money changed into the right kind of shekels. For every coin changed the changers charged one *maah,* which was the equivalent of one penny, and, if the coin presented was larger than a half-shekel and change had to be given, another *maah* was charged for giving change—and remember a *maah* was the equivalent of the quarter of a day's pay. So the pilgrim had to pay his tax, which was the equivalent of nearly two days' pay, and, he might well have to pay another half day's pay to get his coin changed and to receive his change. It was one colossal ramp in which poor pilgrims were being mercilessly fleeced. It brought in between sixteen to eighteen thousand dollars a year, which in modern terms would be millions, and such was the wealth of the Temple treasury that, when Crassus, the Roman general, plundered it in 54 B.C., he took away the equivalent of five million dollars, and that did not exhaust it. The modern purchasing power of such a sum would be in the category of hundreds of milions of dollars. The pilgrims were being victimized by the money-changers.

The others involved were the pigeon-sellers. Almost all the visitors to the Temple would make some offering or other, and for the poorer people the commonest victim was the pigeon or

e. A sacrificial victim had to be without spot or blemish, ...e Temple authorities had appointed inspectors to see that ...ms were perfect. It was possible for a pilgrim to buy his ...geons outside the Temple; there were shops where they were on sale. But all the likelihood was that the inspector would find a blemish. So it was safer to buy the victims at the Temple shops where they had already been inspected. Outside the Temple a pair of pigeons could cost as little as five cents, but inside the Temple they could cost as much as $1.50. Here was a still more lucrative racket, and the shops in the Court of the Gentiles, where the trading went on, were called the Bazaars of Annas.

So then we see why Jesus was enraged. Poor pilgrims were being fleeced. The one place where the Gentile could worship was turned into a shouting, arguing, bargaining oriental market. And we can see why Annas and company hated Jesus; their vested interest had been attacked. Put into its background, the cleansing of the Temple becomes vividly meaningful.

Insofar as it is possible every Bible incident should be read against its background. This often means work and research in order to understand—but the result is worth it.

There is another fact which often has a large part to play in our interpretation of the Bible, especially in the case of the Old Testament. The Jew knew nothing of secondary causes. The Jew in Old Testament times attributed everything to the direct action of God. In modern times, if there is thunder, we explain the thunder by certain atmospheric conditions. The Jew says quite simply: "God thundered," or, "God sent the thunder." If the crops are destroyed by blasting and mildew, we explain it by soil conditions and by the action of pests. The Jew says: "God sent blasting and mildew." Modern man would explain plague and pestilence by telling of the conditions which caused them. The Jew would simply say: "God sent the plague or the pestilence."

There is one vivid example of this in 2 Kings 19:35, 36. The story comes from the invasion of Palestine by Sennacherib the King of Assyria. He had besieged Jerusalem, and all seemed lost. It seemed but a matter of time until there would be nothing for it but for the city to surrender. And then there come the two verses:

And that night the angel of the Lord went forth and slew a hundred and eighty-five thousand in the camp of the Assyrians; and when men arose early in the morning, behold, these were all dead bodies. Then

Sennacherib king of Assyria departed, and went home an... Nineveh.

It so happens that this is a piece of history of which we have ... other accounts. The first is in the Greek historian Herodotus, who tells us that the King of Assyria retreated because mice gnawed the strings of the bows and the thongs of the shields of his army. The angel of the Lord or mice? The third account is from a Chaldean historian called Berosus, who says that Sennacherib was compelled to retreat because pestilence decimated his army. The angel of the Lord—mice—pestilence—which was it? Which account is true? Surely the answer is—all of them. It was plague which caused the army to retreat—so Berosus is right. Plague, especially bubonic plague, is carried by rats and mice—so Herodotus is right. It was not the will of God that Sennacherib and his hosts should conquer Jerusalem—therefore the Hebrew historian is right. The pagan historians fixed on the secondary causes of Sennacherib's retreat; the Hebrew historian eliminated the secondary cause and went straight to God.

This is something which we have to remember especially when we read the Old Testament. The Old Testament moves in a world that is full of God. Events are always being attributed to the direct action of God instead of to the secondary cause. The result is that in the Old Testament many a thing is regarded as miraculous of which we now know the secondary cause. It might well be said that the Jew knew *that* God did things; we know more of *how* he does them.

Still another important point for interpretation emerges. There are parts of the Old Testament which are poetry and to treat them as prose is to misunderstand them and to do them injustice.

We take one outstanding example of that, Joshua 10:12, 13:

> Then spoke Joshua to the Lord in the day when the Lord gave the
> Amorites over to the men of Israel; and he said in the sight of Israel,
> "Sun, stand thou still at Gibeon,
> and thou Moon in the valley of Aijalon."
> And the sun stood still, and the moon stayed,
> until the nation took vengeance on their enemies.

This is clearly a passage at which we would have to look with some care, in order to arrive at a correct interpretation of it.

...thing that strikes us about it is that it cannot in any ...e taken literally for the very simple and sufficient reason ...he sun does not in fact move; the sun always stands still. It ...e earth which moves, and if at any time the earth had ceased ...move, then life as we know it would have come suddenly and catastrophically to an end. Further, if anything resembling this had somehow or other happened, if there had been an occasion when it could be said that the sun or the earth stood still, then this would be an event, not simply of Jewish history, but also of world history, and there would be some record or memory of it in the history of every nation in the world. It is not possible to approach this with a crude literalism.

But then we note something else about it. It is a quotation from the Book of Jashar (Joshua 10:13). This Book of Jashar is quoted again. It is quoted as the origin of David's great lament over the death of Saul (2 Samuel 1:18). And so the fact becomes clear that the Book of Jashar is in fact a book of poetry, and the material that is in it is poetry. The Revised Standard Version prints the Joshua story as poetry and correctly so.

So then in this passage we have a poet speaking. The poet here speaks of the sun in the same kind of way as the poet of Psalm 19, who speaks of the sun daily leaving his chamber like a bridegroom and running his daily race from one end of the heavens to the other (Psalm 19:5, 6). This is the language of poetry; it is even the language we use in everyday life. We say of an occasion: "It was the longest half hour that I spent in all my life," but all half hours are thirty minutes, neither more nor less. We say of a golden day: "Never did the time pass more quickly," but the time always passes at the same rate.

So we need not worry trying to find explanations of the Joshua passage. It means that by the help of God that day was long enough for the victory to be won, that into it there were by the grace of God packed these events which gave victory to God's people Israel. We do the Bible an ill service when we turn the beauty of its poetry into prose.

We come now to what may well be the most important single thing to remember when we are seeking to interpret the Bible. It took all of one thousand years to write the Bible, and the period of history covered in the Bible—apart from the parts of the Bible which deal with the things which happened before

history can be said to have begun—amounts to somet
three thousand years. Take one thousand years in n
terms. Go back a thousand years, and we arrive somew
about the time of Alfred the Great. Clearly, life and thoug.
and society and civilization were very different one thousane
years ago. It is so with the Bible. If the Bible story stretches over
scores of centuries, there cannot be in it one flat level of thought
and religion and ethics. There is bound to be development. God
could only tell men what men were able and willing to receive.
God's message to men had to be adapted to the state of men's
minds when that message was given. If we are going to teach a
boy algebra, we do not start with the binomial theorem; we lead
slowly up to it. If we are going to teach a child to play the piano,
we do not start with Bach's preludes and fugues; they are a
summit, not a beginning. If we are going to teach a boy Greek,
we do not start with the odes of Pindar, or the choruses of
Aeschylus; something much easier has to be the beginning. It is
so with the Bible. God had to lead the minds of men from less to
more, from lower to higher levels, from the glimmerings to the
full blaze. This is obvious, for, if men knew it all already why
should the great prophets come, and above all why should Jesus
come? Revelation is an ongoing process all the time.

Very commonly this is called the principle of *developing
revelation.* God's revelation, so to say, developed with man's
ability to receive it. It would be better to speak, not of a
developing revelation, but rather of a *developing grasp of revelation.*
It is not so much that God doled out his revelation in small
doses; it is rather that he was offering the blaze of truth all the
time, but the mind of man was capable of and willing to receive
only a limited amount of it.

When we find in the Bible things which are sub-Christian,
there is no need to defend them, and there is no need to explain
them away. They represent the stage to which men had reached
at that particular time. This we know, because Jesus more than
once said: "You have heard that it was said . . . But I say to you"
(Matthew 5:21, 27, 31, 33, 38, 43). We accept this in practice, for
there are few or no Christians who live out all the ceremonial
laws of the Old Testament. We know that with Jesus Christ
these have been left behind. It is not that they were wrong; it is
not that they were in error. But that they were incomplete.
Behind every one of them there is a great and unchanging
truth, and these old laws are imperfect grasps of that truth.

...resent what men made of that truth at that particular
...Ve can see this in many things in the Bible, but we shall
...ate it, first, by looking at certain religious practices, and,
...ond at certain religious principles in which there has been
...evelopment.

1. Let us look first at the answer to the question, *How do I show my religion?* as that question is answered in the legal parts of the Old Testament.

(a) The Jew showed his religion by abstaining from certain kinds of food. As everyone knows the Jew would not, and will not, eat pigs' flesh. "And the swine . . . is unclean to you. Of their flesh you shall not eat, and their carcasses you shall not touch; they are unclean to you" (Leviticus 11:7, 8). That is laid down as a law in Leviticus, but it does not stop us eating bacon for breakfast, or a pork chop for dinner.

(b) The Jew showed his religion by wearing the tasselled cloak, the phylacteries or prayer boxes, and by putting the *mezuzah,* the little cylindrical wooden fixture with words of Scripture in it on his doorpost. The phylacteries were little leather boxes with certain texts written in parchment inside them, and were strapped to the wrist and the forehead at prayer.

> The Lord said to Moses: Speak to the people of Israel, and bid them to make tassels on the corners of their garments. . . . And it shall be to you a tassel to look upon and remember all the commandments of the Lord. (Numbers 15:37-39)

> And these words which I command you this day shall be upon your heart . . . and you shall bind them as a sign upon your hand, and they shall be as frontlets between your eyes (phylacteries), and you shall write them on the doorposts of your house, and on your gates *(mezuzah).* (Deuteronomy 6:6-9)

The Jew still wears his tasselled prayer shawl and his phylacteries at prayer; he still fixes the *mezuzah* to the door of his house or flat. But the Christian does not consider these commandments in any way binding upon him.

(c) Above all the Jew showed his religion by circumcision. This was the sign of the covenant. This was the sign that he was a member of the people of God. So important is it that it is said, "Any uncircumcised male, who is not circumcised in the flesh of his foreskin, shall be cut off from his people; he has broken my

covenant" (Genesis 17:14). But no Christian accep
obligation of circumcision.

The Jew shows his religion by abstention from certain foo
by the wearing of certain objects, by affixing certain things to h.
house, and by circumcision. Let no one belittle these things;
they are a public demonstration of the faith of the Jew, and it
would be a good thing if Christians showed their faith as openly.
But this is the way in which a Christian shows his religion: "By
this all men will know that you are my disciples, if you have love
for one another" (John 13:35).

In the Old Testament there are ways of showing a man's
religion—and they are honorable ways. They grasp the fact that
man must show his faith, but they have not reached the full
revelation that a man must show his faith by his love. This had to
wait for Jesus.

2. Next, let us look at the answer to the question, *How do I
protect my religion?* How do I keep it safe from any infection
which would make it less pure?

It is in the answer to this question that we find some of these
things which fill us with horror as we read. In the event of war if
a city surrenders, then its inhabitants are to be put to forced
labor.

> But if it makes no peace with you, but makes war against you, then
> you shall besiege it; and when the Lord your God gives it into your
> hand, you shall put all its males to the sword, but the women and the
> little ones, the cattle and everything else in the city, all its spoil, you
> shall take as booty for yourselves. . . . But in the cities of these peoples
> that the Lord your God gives you for an inheritance, you shall save
> alive nothing that breathes, but you shall utterly destroy them.
> (Deuteronomy 20:12-17)

The instructions are followed at the siege of Jericho and the
result is: "Then they utterly destroyed all in the city, both men
and women, young and old, oxen, sheep and asses, with the
edge of the sword" (Joshua 6:21).

In the war with Amalek Samuel's instructions from God to
Saul are: "Now go and smite Amalek, and utterly destroy all that
they have; do not spare them, but kill both man and woman,
infant and suckling, ox and sheep, camel and ass" (1 Samuel
15:3). It sounds, and it is, so bloodthirsty. But what must be
remembered is this—in this there was no personal hatred, there
was no blood lust, there was no murderous passion for

111

er. What was behind it was this—all foreign faiths were
ection; they were a threat to the purity of the worship of
weh; and everything to do with them had for safety's and for
urity's sake to be wiped out. This is actually said, for the
instructions in Deuteronomy conclude with the words which
give the reason for all this, "that they may not teach you to do
according to all their abominable practices which they have
done in the service of their gods, and so to sin against the Lord
your God" (Deuteronomy 20:18). The whole point is that these
foreign nations were idolaters, and were therefore the enemies
of God, and therefore had to be wiped out lest the infection of
their heathen practices taint the purity of Hebrew religion.

But when Jesus comes, we get a new conception. We get the
conception that we are not to wipe out God's enemies by killing
them; we are to wipe them out by converting them. In the
American civil war over slavery Abraham Lincoln was charged
with being far too gracious and kindly to the southern states.
"They are your enemies," people said to him, "and it is your task
to destroy them." Lincoln answered: "Do I not destroy my
enemies when I make them my friends?" The Old Testament
had got hold of half of a great truth, the truth that the enemies
of God must be destroyed. But we have to wait for Jesus to
discover that the way to destroy the enemies of God is to convert
them so that they become the friends of God.

3. The third question which it is natural to ask is, *What is it that
I ought to give to God?* What gift can I take to him to please him?

There is a great part of the Old Testament which is all about
the sheep and lambs and calves and bulls and oxen and doves
and pigeons and wine and flour and oil which form part of the
ceremonial sacrifices to God. The theory behind this is quite
clear. The worshiper says to himself: "I must give to God my
most precious possession," and in an agricultural society his
most precious possession was the animals and the crops over
which he had toiled.

But even in the Old Testament itself the inadequacy of this is
seen. Isaiah hears God say:

> What to me is the multitude of your sacrifices?
>   says the Lord
> I have had enough of burnt offerings of rams
>   and the fat of fed beasts;
> I do not delight in the blood of bulls,
>   or of lambs, or of he-goats.

When you come to appear before me
   who requires of you
   this trampling of my courts?
Bring no more vain offerings;
   incense is an abomination to me . . .
Wash yourselves; make yourselves clean;
   remove the evil of your doings
   from before my eyes;
cease to do evil;
   learn to do good;
seek justice;
   correct oppression;
defend the fatherless,
   plead for the widow. (Isaiah 1:11-13, 16-17)

As Isaiah saw it, the whole paraphernalia of sacrifice was one vast irrelevance. Micah said the same.

With what shall I come before the Lord,
   and bow myself before God on high?
Shall I come before him with burnt-offerings,
   with calves a year old?
Will the Lord be pleased with thousands of rams,
   with ten thousands of rivers of oil?
Shall I give my first-born for my transgression,
   the fruit of my body for the sin of my soul?
He hath showed you, O man, what is good,
   and what does the Lord require of you
but to do justice, and to love kindness,
   and to walk humbly with your God? (Micah 6:6-8)

And it is in Hosea that we find what looks as if it was Jesus' favorite text. "For I desire steadfast love and not sacrifice" (Hosea 6:6; Matthew 9:13; 12:7).

It is clear God never wanted the sacrifice of animals. The Jews thought he did, because they saw in these animals their most precious possession, and to God they were willing to give them. But the prophets saw the irrelevance of animal sacrifice, and Jesus above all saw it. The most precious thing a man has is his heart, his self, a heart and a self filled with love for God and love for man—that is the only gift God wants.

So in the Old Testament we see time and time again that a great truth is grasped, but it is imperfectly grasped. For the full grasp we have to wait for Jesus. It is not that the Old Testament is wrong—far from that; it is an essential stage to that goal which is Jesus Christ.

Let us now take two of the very great conceptions of the Christian faith and let us see how they develop throughout the Bible, until they culminate in Jesus Christ.

First, let us take the conception of *the forgiveness of our enemies and of those who have injured us*.

1. In the beginning so far from any desire to forgive there was a cry for unlimited vengeance. Genesis 4:23, 24 is one of the oldest fragments in the Bible, and in it the cry is for vengeance:

> Lamech said to his wives:
> Adah and Zillah, hear my voice;
> you wives of Lamech, hearken to what I say:
> I have slain a man for wounding me,
> a young man for striking me.
> If Cain is avenged sevenfold,
> truly Lamech seventy-sevenfold.

It is Lamech's boast that he has exacted vengeance for injury. He has killed a man for injuring him, and his desire is for a vengeance which will exceed the injury seventy-sevenfold. Here in the most primitive of all passages there is no thought of forgiveness, only for vengeance.

2. The next stage is a stage at which the Old Testament has often been, and still is, much misunderstood. It is often said that the Old Testament believes in "an eye for an eye, and a tooth for a tooth," and this is claimed to be one of "the bloodthirsty laws of the Old Testament."

> If any harm follows, then you shall give life for life, eye for eye, tooth for tooth, hand for hand, foot for foot, burn for burn, wound for wound, stripe for stripe. (Exodus 21:23-25)

> When a man causes a disfigurement in his neighbour, as he has done, it shall be done to him, fracture for fracture, eye for eye, tooth for tooth; as he has disfigured a man, he shall be disfigured. He who kills a beast shall make it good, and he who kills a man shall be put to death. (Leviticus 24:19-21)

> Your eye shall not pity; it shall be life for life, eye for eye, tooth for tooth, hand for hand, foot for foot. (Deuteronomy 19:21)

To call these bloodthirsty laws is totally to misunderstand them; they are the precise reverse of that.

In the early days the vendetta or blood feud was typical of tribal society. In the vendetta, if any man injured a member of another tribe, it was the duty of all the members of the injured man's tribe to take all possible vengeance on all the members of the tribe of the man who injured him. And thus a comparatively slight injury could lead to a war between two tribes in which many lives were lost. These laws which we have just quoted were the first attempt to *limit* vengeance. If vengeance was to be taken, it must be only to the precise extent to which injury had been inflicted, and no longer must injury issue in a bloodthirsty tribal war.

In later times this law of precise retribution became modified. Suppose a man's tooth is knocked out, and the tooth is a decayed tooth, it will be unjust to knock out in retribution a tooth which is a healthy tooth. Suppose the eye which was injured to be a very inefficient eye, it will be wrong to knock out in revenge a perfectly healthy eye. So each injury came to be assessed at a money penalty, and not as a physical exchange of injuries. But the main point is that here there is the first step toward the controlled limitation of vengeance, and it is therefore a very big step in the right direction.

3. At the third stage we arrive at a stage when forgiveness and non-retaliation are urged, but with certain limitations and for certain conditions.

(a) Forgiveness is urged, with the limitation that it is to extend only to fellow Hebrews.

> You shall not hate your brother in your heart, but you shall reason with your neighbour, lest you bear sin because of him. You shall not take vengeance nor bear any grudge against the sons of your own people, but you shall love your neighbour as yourself; I am the Lord. (Leviticus 19:17, 18)

This is definite enough but the forgiveness is limited to "your brother," and to "the sons of your own people." It does not necessarily extend to the Gentile.

(b) Forgiveness is urged, because vengeance belongs to God, and if a man's cause is just, he can leave the vengeance to God:

> Do not say, I will repay evil.
> Wait for the Lord and he will help you. (Proverbs 20:22)

The same atitude is seen in the intertestamental book *The Testament of the Twelve Patriarchs:*

> Love one another from the heart; and if a man sins against you, cast forth the poison of hate and speak peaceably to him, and retain no guile in your soul. And if he confesses and repents, forgive him. . . . And if he is shameless and persists in his wrong-doing, even so forgive him from the heart, and leave the avenging to God. (The Testament of Gad 6:3, 7)

True, forgiveness is urged, but God will exercise the vengeance for the good man.

(c) Most commonly of all, forgiveness is urged in order to win the favor of God:

> If your enemy is hungry, give him bread to eat,
>   and if he is thirsty, give him water to drink;
> for you will heap coals of fire on his head,
>   and the Lord will reward you. (Proverbs 25:21)

> Do not rejoice when your enemy falls,
>   and let not your heart be glad when he stumbles;
> lest the Lord see it, and be displeased,
>   and turn away his anger from him. (Proverbs 24:17, 18)

Even a passage like Lamentations 3:30, "Let him give his cheek to the smiter, / and be filled with insults," derives from the fact that "The Lord is good to those who wait for him, to the soul that seeks him" (Lamentations 3:25).

It is the same with a passage from Ecclesiasticus 28:2:

> Forgive your neighbour the wrong he has done,
> and then your sins will be pardoned when you pray.

So again, "If anyone seeks to do evil to you, do good to him, and pray for him, and then you shall be redeemed by the Lord from all evil" (The Testament of Joseph 18:2).

One of the few Old Testament passages on forgiveness in which there is no limitation and no condition is Proverbs 24:29:

> Do not say, "I will do to him as he has done to me:
> I will pay the man back for what he has done."

So then the Old Testament begins with unlimited vengeance; it moves on to a strictly controlled exchange of penalty; it moves still further on to the urging of forgiveness, but within certain limits and conditions.

4. And so finally we come to Jesus. The essence of the teaching of Jesus on forgiveness is in the Sermon on the Mount:

> You have heard that it was said, "An eye for an eye, and a tooth for a tooth." But I say to you, Do not resist one who is evil. But if anyone strikes you on the right cheek, turn to him the other also. . . . You have heard that it was said, You shall love your neighbour and hate your enemy. But I say to you, Love your enemies and pray for those who persecute you, so that you may be sons of your Father who is in heaven; for he makes his sun rise on the evil and on the good, and sends rain on the just and on the unjust. For if you love those who love you, what reward have you? Do not even the tax-collectors do the same? And if you salute only your brethren, what more are you doing than others? Do not even the Gentiles do the same? You, therefore, must be perfect, as your heavenly Father is perfect. (Matthew 5:38-48)

There are no limitations and no conditions. Forgiveness is absolute. There is a reward, but the reward is that he who forgives becomes like God. As Paul put it, "Be kind to one another, tenderhearted, forgiving one another, as God in Christ forgave you" (Ephesians 4:32). So the wheel has gone full circle; it began with unlimited vengeance, and it ends in Christ with unlimited forgiveness. (Contrast Christ's seventy times seven, Matthew 18:22, with Genesis 4:24.) On this matter we have to say unequivocally, "It is not by the Old Testament but by the New Testament, not by the Law but by the Gospel, not by anyone other than Jesus Christ, that I judge my duty to forgive." So when people quote the Old Testament to us, we have to say quite frankly, "This is the stage which at that time men had reached. This is the part of God's revelation which they had grasped. But the full revelation is in Jesus Christ, and we take our orders and our pattern from no one but him."

The second great idea at which we must look is *life after death*. We shall look at the development of that idea throughout the Bible.

1. In the earliest times the Hebrews had no real belief in any life after death. They believed that the souls of all who died went to Sheol or Hades. Sheol is not hell; Sheol was the place of all the dead. It was a gray, shadowy land, from which all the color and the strength and the meaning had been evacuated. It was separated from man and from God alike, and the souls who lived there lived a ghostly, specter-like existence. It was not

extinction, but it was no more than the shadow of life. Again
and again this hopelessness comes out in the Old Testament.

For in death there is no remembrance of thee;
  in Sheol who can give thee praise? (Psalm 6:5)

What profit is there in my death,
  if I go down to the Pit?
Will the dust praise thee?
  Will it tell of my faithfulness? (Psalm 30:9)

Look away from me, that I may know gladness.
  before I depart and be no more! (Psalm 39:13)

For my soul is full of troubles
  and my life draws near to Sheol.
I am reckoned among those who go down to the Pit;
  I am a man who has no strength,
like one forsaken among the dead,
  like the slain that lie in the grave,
like those whom thou dost remember no more,
  for they are cut off from thy hand . . .
  Dost thou work wonders for the dead?
  Do the shades rise up to praise thee?
Is thy steadfast love declared in the grave?
  or thy faithfulness in Abaddon?
Are thy wonders known in the darkness,
  or thy saving help in the land of forgetfulness?
              (Psalm 88:3-12)

The dead do not praise the Lord,
  nor do any that go down into silence (Psalm 115:17)

For the fate of the sons of men and the fate of beasts is the same; as
one dies, so dies the other. They all have the same breath, and man
has no advantage over the beasts; for all is vanity. All go to one place;
all are from the dust and all turn to dust again. (Ecclesiastes 3:19, 20)

He who is joined with all the living has hope, for a living dog is better
than a dead lion. For the living know that they will die, but the dead
know nothing, and they have no more reward; but the memory of
them is lost. . . Whatever your hand finds to do, do it with your
might; for there is no work or thought or knowledge of wisdom in
Sheol to which you are going. (Ecclesiastes 9:4-10)

For Sheol cannot thank thee,
  death cannot praise thee;
those who go down to the pit cannot hope
  for thy faithfulness. (Isaiah 38:18)

For there is hope for a tree,
  if it be cut down, that it will sprout again,
  and that its shoots will not cease.
Though its root grow old in the earth,
  and its stump die in the ground,
yet at the scent of water it will bud
  and put forth branches like a young plant.
But man dies, and is laid low;
  man breathes his last, and where is he?
As waters fail from a lake,
  and a river wastes away and dries up,
so man lies down, and rises not again;
  till the heavens are no more he will not awake,
  or be roused out of his sleep. (Job 14:7-12)

It is clear that in the Old Testament there is little to hope for after death—a land of shadows, a land of the dark, a land of silence, a land of forgetfulness, a land which is cut off from God and from men. J. E. McFadyen wrote in *The Message of Israel* (p. 46); "There are few more wonderful things than this in the long story of religion, that for centuries men lived the noblest lives, doing their duties and bearing their sorrows, without hope of future reward; and they did this because in all their going out and coming in they were very sure of God." Then McFadyen went on to say: "An American scholar has said that "it has never been possible for man, thinking man, on a basis of *this life only*, to make life anything but meaningless nonsense." The Old Testament is the triumphant refutation of such an assertion." In the earliest form of Hebrew religion there was no belief in any real life beyond the grave and on the other side of death.

2. But this is not the end of the matter in the Old Testament. In the Old Testament there are many passages which are at least on the way to a belief in life after death. Isaiah can say:

Thy dead shall live, their bodies shall rise.
  O dwellers in the dust, awake and sing for joy!
For thy dew is a dew of light,
  and on the land of the shades thou wilt let it fall.
          (Isaiah 26:19)

In Daniel we find the belief:

And many of those who sleep in the dust of the earth shall awake, some to everlasting life, and some to shame and everlasting contempt. And those who are wise shall shine like the brightness of the firmament; and those who turn many to righteousness, like the stars for ever and ever. (Daniel 12:2, 3)

Let us trace the process and the reasons by which the real belief in life after death came into being.

(a) The greater men's conception of God, the more they came to be certain that there was no part of the universe outside the being of God. When men thought of their God as only the god of their nation, and when they were willing to grant that each nation had its own god, then the area of God's power was strictly limited; but when they moved on to believe in only one God, the God of all men and all nations and all possible worlds, then they could not avoid thinking of him also as the God of that world which came after death.

> Whither shall I go from thy Spirit?
>   Or whither shall I flee from thy presence?
> If I ascend to heaven, thou art there!
> If I make my bed in Sheol, thou art there!
>   (Psalm 139:7, 8)

Once men began to believe in one God of all the universe, then this life and any other life are in the presence of God, and the idea of Sheol was bound to change.

(b) Sometimes men's glimpse of a life to come was like a leap in the dark. It was not a settled belief to begin with. It was something which a man grasped like a life-belt in a sea of trouble. It was that way with Job. We have already quoted Job's words of despair, and Job could despair:

> As the cloud fades and vanishes,
>   so he who goes down to Sheol does not come up.
>   (7:9)

But Job felt that it would make all the difference in the world if he could only hope for something. As Galloway once said, "The enigmas of life become at least less baffling, when we come to rest in the thought that this is not the last act of the human drama." So Moffatt translates Job's hope:

> If only man might die and live again,
>   I could endure my weary post until relief arrived;

thou wouldst call, and I would come,
    when thou didst yearn for life that thou hadst made.
                (14:14,15)

So in Job's heart there was the longing—if only there was something still to come! And then suddenly he makes the leap:

I know that my Redeemer lives,
    and at last he will stand upon the earth;
and after my skin has been thus destroyed,
    then from my flesh I shall see God,
whom I shall see on my side,
    and my eyes shall behold and not another.
                (19:25-27)

It is not a settled doctrine; it is not a reasoned faith; it is not part of a creed. It is the first leap in the dark to grasp at God, not just in this life, but forever.

(c) Sometimes that belief in the life to come came not from any sudden leap, but from the growing conviction that a relationship, a connection, a friendship, a link established with God is in its essence unbreakable, just because God is God. So the man who had found God in this world believed that, since God is always God, you cannot lose him. To say that love is immortal would mean the same thing. So the psalmists write:

Nevertheless I am continually with thee;
    thou dost hold my right hand.
Thou dost guide me with thy counsel
    and afterward thou wilt receive me to glory.
Whom have I in heaven but thee?
    And there is nothing on earth that I desire besides thee.
My flesh and my heart may fail,
    but God is the strength of my heart,
        and my portion for ever. (Psalm 73:23-26)

I keep the Lord always before me;
    because he is at my right hand,
        I shall not be moved.
Therefore my heart is glad, and my soul rejoices;
    my body also dwells secure.
For thou dost not give me up to Sheol,
    or let thy godly one see the Pit.
Thou dost show me the path of life;
    in thy presence there is fullness of joy,

> in thy right hand are pleasures for evermore.
> (Psalm 16:8-11)

In these two passages there is the confidence of a heart which has established a connection with God which it is convinced cannot be terminated by death.

(d) But perhaps that which most of all brought to the Hebrews a real belief in a life to come was simply the fact that, unless they brought another world into the scheme of things, then neither God's promises to the nation nor to the individual would ever be fulfilled. There was a time when men looked for God's rewards and punishments within this present time scheme. The psalmist said:

> I have been young, and now am old;
> yet I have not seen the righteous forsaken.
> or his children begging bread. (Psalm 37:25)

But it became less and less possible to say that. The good man might die in agony in the cruelty of the persecutor. The man of principle was so often—as he still is—the man the world hates. Israel was the chosen people, but Israel was a nation subjugated by the Assyrians, the Babylonians, the Persians, the Greeks, the Romans. The plain fact was that without a life to come it was impossible to believe in either the love or the justice of God. In the famous phrase, the new world was called in to redress the balance of the old. Thus between the Testaments this belief in a life to come became strong, so that those who had been true to God might find their reward and that the promises of God might yet be fulfilled.

> They that fear the Lord shall arise to eternal life; their life shall be in light, and it will never cease. (Psalms of Solomon 3:12)

> After that, when the time of the Advent of the Messiah is completed, he shall return in glory into the heavens. And then shall all those arise who slept with their hope in him. (Apocalypse of Baruch 30:1)

Since God's man never received God's blessing in this distressful life, men were driven to believe in the life to come.

3. But at the best this was a hope, and not till the coming of Jesus does the hope turn to certainty. It is the word of Jesus.

> In my Father's house are many rooms; if it were not so, would I have told you that I go to prepare a place for you? And when I go and

prepare a place for you, I will come again and will take you to myself, that where I am you may be also. . . . Because I live you will live also. (John 14:2, 3, 19)

As Paul sees it, the Christian certainty of the life to come comes from the fact that the Christian's Savior is one who was dead and is alive again. "As in Adam all die, so also in Christ shall all be made alive" (1 Corinthians 15:22). In Jesus Christ what had been a hope became a certainty, and what had been a theory became a fact. And so within the Bible we see the belief in the life to come developing from the gray shadowy Sheol to life forever with the Lord. And once again, when people quote the grim parts of the Old Testament where belief in the life to come does not in any real way exist, then we do not need to defend these parts, and we do not need to explain them away. Once again we can say, "Yes, that is as far as men had reached at that time. But that is not the Christian belief. These are only steps on the way to the conviction of life in Christ here and hereafter."

There is one more big demand on us in our study of the Bible. To understand any book we have to try to enter into the mind and the heart and the life and the circumstances of the person who wrote it. We have to try to see how his mind works; we have to try to understand his general world view. This is just as true of the Bible as of any other book. We must try to enter into the mind of the people who wrote it. To go to the Bible with the eyes and the ideas and the preconceptions of a twentieth-century western man is the surest way to misunderstand it. We have to try to think ourselves into the mind of a man of the date at which each book was written. And we have continually to remind ourselves what the object of the writers of the Bible was in writing at all. Their one object was to show the ways of God with men; their one aim was to show life in terms of the sovereignty of God. Their aim was exclusively religious. They were not writing history; they knew no more of scientific history than any of their contemporaries did. They were not writing science; their science was as primitive as that of their age. Their aim was to show God in action.

There is nothing at all unnatural in this. A man is always an expert within an area. My mother knew no Hebrew and no Greek and no theology, but she was the greatest saint I ever knew. I would never have gone to her for the translation of a word or for the expounding of a doctrine; but I would have gone to her every time to learn how to live with God as a constant companion. So in the Bible I do not look in the first place for history; I do not look at all for science; but I do look for God—and I find him. Let us then see some of the things which we must remember, if we are to enter into the minds of the biblical writers.

1. They have a quite different view of the world. For them the earth was the fixed center of things, and the sun emerged each day to run his daily race across the heavens (Psalm 19:4, 5). The earth is like a flat plate sitting on the waters with the solid dome of the firmament overarching it, across which the great lights of the sun and moon traveled and which opened for the waters above to make the rain (Genesis 1:1-19). But the important thing is not what they believed the earth to be like; the important thing is what they believed man to be like, and what they believed God to be like, and that they were quite certain that, whatever the earth is like, the creating power of God is behind it.

2. They have a quite different view of sickness. They attributed sickness to the demons or to the sin of the sick person. It was not only mental illness that they ascribed to the demons. Any part of the body might, as they thought, be occupied and rendered ill by a demon. All illness, so they believed, had some sin behind it.

We no longer attribute illness to the demons or necessarily to the sin of the sick person himself. But in one way these ancient thinkers were curiously modern. What we have been saying is that, in the modern term, they believed illness to be psychosomatic. *Psychê* is the Greek for *soul,* and *sôma* is the Greek for *body.* And to say that illness is psychosomatic means that it has more than a physical cause; it has its spiritual causes as well. It may indeed have no physical cause, only a physical effect. This means that it is never enough to concentrate on man as a body, but that he has a spirit as well, and the body will never be healthy until the spirit also is whole. Healing—and in their own way the ancient writers saw this—is always more than a physical matter.

3. They have quite a different way of thinking, and this is the most important and the most difficult point of all. Among the

Hebrews in biblical times there were few—perhaps none—who thought, or could think in abstract terms and abstract arguments. *They thought in pictures.* Now, the pictures in which they thought were bound to be the pictures of their own time, the pictures which were part of the scene of day-to-day living in their own day, for the simple reason that these were the only pictures which the people of their day could understand. So, then, inevitably what happens to us is that we are confronted with a piece of timeless truth enclosed in a quite local and temporary picture. I time and time again our task is to penetrate beyond the husk of the picture to the kernel of the truth.

This process has a name—and it is a name which very unfortunately and very unfairly has become to many people a bad word. It is called *demythologizing.* The trouble about this is that the word *myth (mythos)* means one thing in Greek and another in English. In English a myth is a piece of fiction, and to say that a thing is mythical is well nigh the same as to say that it is untrue. But in Greek a myth is a story designed to make clear some truth which it is difficult or impossible to put into plain language which an ordinary man can follow. A myth is truth in a picture.

There is, for instance, the famous myth in the sixth book of Plato's *Republic.* There is a cave, and in it there are men so fettered that they can look only inward. In front of them there is a wall, and they can look only at the wall. Behind them there is a raised path, and behind that there is a bright light of a burning fire. People and things are always passing along the path between the fire and the backs of the fettered men, and the shadows of the people and the things are continually thrown on the wall in front. Inevitably men bound in a position like that would come to think that the shadows were the realities, because they were so fettered that they could not see the real objects at all; and, if all their lives men had been so fettered, even if they were freed, it would be hard to convince them that the shadows were unreal and that the real people and things were the realities. This is a myth, and it is designed to show how men become so attached to the shadows of life that they become incapable of seeing the realities. That is the Greek idea of myth. A myth is a story constructed to demonstrate and illustrate and bring home a truth, which would have no impact upon men, if it was expressed in abstract language.

Time and time again our task in studying the Bible is to get at the timeless truth at the back of the temporary picture. The twentieth-century scholars were far from being the first to recognize this need. Origen, the great scholar, knew all about it and stated it clearly and forcibly half way through the third century (*De Principiis* 1:16):

> What man of sense will suppose that the first and the second and the third day, and the evening and the morning, existed without a sun and moon and stars? Who is so foolish as to believe that God like a farmer planted a garden in Eden, and placed in it a tree of life, that might be seen and touched, so that one who has tasted of the fruit by his bodily lips obtained life? Or again, that one was partaker of good and evil by eating that which was taken from a tree? And if God is said to have walked in a garden in the evening, and Adam to have hidden under a tree, I do not suppose that anyone doubts that these things figuratively indicate certain mysteries, the history being apparently but not literally true. . . . Nay, the Gospels themselves are filled with the same kind of narratives. Take, for example, the story of the Devil taking Jesus up into a high mountain to show him from thence the kingdoms of the world and the glory of them: what thoughtful reader would not condemn those who teach that it was with the eye of the body—which needs a lofty height that even the near neighbourhood may be seen—that Jesus beheld the kingdoms of the Persians, and Scythians, and Indians, and Parthians, and the manner in which their rulers were glorified among men?

Origen begins by noting that in the creation story it is three times said that there was evening and morning *before* the sun and moon were created (Genesis 1:5, 8, 13, 14). What Origen is saying is that here we have truth, but truth in a picture. The picture is the husk; the truth is the kernel. Let us take briefly the three stories to which Origen refers.

(a) There is the creation story, or rather there are two different creation stories. If you ask any intelligent schoolboy to put into one sentence what Genesis 1 and 2 are saying, he will at once answer: "They are saying that God made the world." That *is* the answer. The *method* by which he made it is not in question. The *fact* that God's creating power is behind this universe and is responsible for this universe is the kernel, however that creating power was exercised.

(b) There is the story of the Fall in Genesis 3. This story is in fact the story of *the fall of every man*. It is worthwhile noting that the name Adam is not a proper name at all; it is in fact the Hebrew word for *man*. This is everyman's story. The man who wrote it would not even know that there was such a word as *psychology,* but there never was written a story more psychologically true than this one. Take it step by step.

1) God gives a command.

2) There comes the temptation to break it. Sin always implies that we know better than God; it is putting our wish above God's will.

3) The wrong thing is attractive (verse 6). It looks good; it was good to eat; to take it would be to win something apparently well worthwhile. Sin is always attractive. If I can only have this, I will be happy. If the forbidden thing was ugly and repulsive, there would be no power in temptation. Temptation has power, because the forbidden things look attractive and desirable and profitable.

4) Sin is committed and the first instinct is to hide (verse 8). No sooner has a man committed a sin than he wants to hide it from men, to hide it from God, and, if possible, to refuse to look at it himself. And there is no greater folly than thinking that anything can be hidden from God.

5) When confronted with his sin, man's first instinct is to push the blame on to someone else. Adam said, "Don't blame me; blame Eve." Eve said, "Don't blame me; blame the serpent." The sinner blames everyone but himself.

Genesis 3 is a story which was never meant to tell of something which happened in a moment of time. It is the story of what happens to Adam—to man, to every man, to you and to me.

(c) Finally, let us take the story of the temptations of Jesus (Matthew 4:1-11; Luke 4:1-13). Origen was right; there is one thing which should make us stop and think—there is no mountain from which anyone can literally see all the kingdoms of the world. Jesus had gone out into the desert to decide how he was to do the task God had given him to do. Was he to use the way of force, of material things, of sensations, of compromise—or the way of the Cross? All that this story tells was not happening visibly and externally. It was going on in the mind of Jesus. He was fighting the battle with all that was trying to lure him from the way God wanted him to take. If you had seen him during it, you would have seen a man alone—or not alone—with God. Just as temptation comes to us, so it came to him, not physically, visibly, but with the attack in the mind and in the heart.

Always we have to remember as we read the Bible that we are

reading the work of men who thought in pictures. We must never waste time in argument about whether this is literally and physically true or not. It is spiritually forever true, and beyond the husk of story we must find the kernel of truth—and live by it.

There are just three things more to say about reading and studying the Bible.

1. While we should study the Bible in detail, we should often, to get the best of it, read it in long sections. We should, for instance, read Mark's Gospel at a sitting, and see the four act drama—preparation, conflict, tragedy, triumph—opening before us. It is possible sometimes to spend too much time on detail and too little on the panoramic and the dramatic pictures of the whole.

2. However long and however devotedly we study the Bible, there will still be passages which are too difficult and which we cannot understand. A man once came to Spurgeon complaining that there were parts of the Bible he did not understand, and saying that he had stopped reading it. Spurgeon said: "When I am eating a nice bit of fish and come upon a bone, I don't fling the whole fish away; I put the bone at the side of the plate and leave it there; and I go on enjoying the fish." When we come to something in the Bible that, even after study, we still do not understand, then we can leave it and pass on. The day will come, when we may understand; and for the present there is wealth enough and more to be going on with.

3. One last thing—there is everything to be said for regular and systematic reading of the Bible. In his autobiographical study, . . . *And Another Thing,* Howard Spring tells how he got the habit. It was during the war in 1940, when things were at their worst. He went to his desk to work, and he found that he could not concentrate for thinking of the threat to our country. It so happened that very recently someone had given him a copy of Marcus Aurelius' *Meditations.* He picked it up and began to read, and somehow the gallant and astringent Stoic philosophy did something to him. "Thereafter," he said,

I made a practice of beginning the morning not by sitting down at my desk with a mind inflamed by all the surging incertitude of the times, but by standing up and reading erect for half-an-hour or so from Marcus Aurelius. I found it a salutary and strengthening custom . . . In this way I read twice through the *Meditations,* and by then it seemed to me that no day should be begun with a plunge straight into "business," whatever that business might be. A few moments of quietness in the company of a supreme and tranquil mind seemed to pay dividends that would make a company promoter lick his chops. It is so easy to begin the day with a rush through the morning paper and a rush through the morning mail, and then to make a rush at the work in hand, but I now think so foolish and so unnecessary. It is like playing the fiddle before it has been keyed up; it will be off pitch all day.

But Howard Spring did not stop there. He goes on, "After the second reading of the *Meditations,* I began the morning with readings from the Bible, and it was during these readings of a book neglected for a quarter of a century that the central importance of a loving God and love of the brethren took possession of my mind."

Howard Spring found that that daily reading brought a serenity and a strength into life, and through it God took possession of his mind. We too ought to be regular in reading the Bible. Howard Spring, being an author, could do his work at home, and was not the slave of the clock. It may be that for us with a train to catch and an office to get to and a family to live among the morning reading will not be possible, or will at least be very difficult. But the reading can just as well be the last thing at night, and we can go to rest thinking of God and of his ways with men.

If we adopt this method of regular reading, it will not be the best of plans to begin at the beginning of the Bible and to go on to the end. We will be far better to use a carefully prepared scheme of daily readings with comments such as the Bible Reading Fellowship or the International Bible Reading Association offers. In that way our reading will be guided and directed; the difficulties will be explained; the meanings will be brought out; and we will have the sense of being one of a great company reading with us all over the world. To read the Bible with system and with help is the way to get the best out of it, for thus we will get strength for the way, wisdom for our minds, and the love of God for our hearts.

And if we read, what translation shall we use? There are some who are troubled with the large number of translations which exist; but of translations we cannot have too many. No translation can be perfect; words will never come completely out of one language into another. Every translation is another attempt to achieve the impossible, the perfect translation. Every translation has something to offer. Away back about 1560 the Geneva Bible was most popular, but the Bishops' Bible, an official translation, was being planned. John Bodley, the father of the founder of Oxford's famous library, had the patent to print the Geneva Bible, and he wondered if he would be allowed to continue to do so when the new official translation was being planned. Matthew Parker, the Archbishop of Canterbury, had no doubt. It was true, he wrote, that the official volume was being planned, "Yet should it nothing hinder but rather do much good to have diversity of translations and readings." The more the better so that each man might find that which spoke to him, and that the struggle for perfection might go on.

Translations can differ vastly. There is—or was—a series of schoolboy cribs called "Kelly's Keys to the Classics." They are absolutely literal and are not English at all. Here is a paragraph from Sophocles' *Oedipus Coloneus:* it is Oedipus who is speaking:

> O dearest son of Aegeus, exemption from old age and death comes to gods alone. But all-powerful Time brings everything else to confusion. The strength of the earth decays, the strength of the body decays, faith dies and faithlessness arises, and the same spirit no longer exists between friends or between city and city. With some at once and with others later on, what is a source of pleasure becomes bitter, and then again is pleasant.

No doubt with that the schoolboy would gain a passing mark—but the haunting beauty of Sophocles is gone. Here is the same passage in Gilbert Murray's translation:

> Fair Aegeus' son, only to gods on high
> Not to grow old is given, nor yet to die,
> All else is turmoiled by our master, Time.
> Decay is in earth's bloom and manhood's prime,
> Faith dies and unfaith blossoms like a flower,
> And who of men shall find from hour to hour,
> Or in loud cities or the marts thereof,
> Or silent chambers of his own heart's love,
> One wind blows true forever? Soon or late
> Hate shall be love and love veer back to hate.

Here the beauty of the Greek speaks again. It is easy to see how different translations can be.

But, suppose we find a good translation, why not stick to it?

Why the many? There are many reasons. Nothing changes so quickly and so imperceptibly as language—and remember that the New Testament was in the colloquial language of the ordinary people. My way of speaking is not my son's, nor his mine. Again, there are continuous new discoveries. Fifty years ago there were more than six hundred words in the New Testament which were listed as "biblical Greek"; now there are fewer than fifty. There have been continuous discoveries of the letters people wrote and the deeds they drew up and the documents they used. And the words that once were strange have been discovered to be common words, and their meaning has been far more closely fixed. New manuscripts of the New Testament are discovered. We have now at least seventy items of New Testament manuscripts which go back to A.D. 150, which is perhaps two centuries older than any manuscripts scholars could use seventy-five years ago. Language does not stand still, and scholarship does not stand still. And if the Bible is, as we believe it is, the word of God, then nothing but the most accurate translation will do. Translation is a never-ending task. Let a student of the Bible use all the translations he can find—and thank God for them.

Chapter 6
The Inspired Book

What exactly do we mean when we say that the Bible is inspired? Or, to put it in another way, what do we mean when we say that the Bible is the word of God? This is not a question which it is easy to answer, but it is a question which the Christian must face, because on his answer to it depends the place which he will give to the Bible in his life and belief.

We began this book by saying that it is not difficult to prove that the Bible is a unique book, with a unique effect on the lives of men. We shall take only two more examples of that. When Sir Walter Scott was dying, he asked his son-in-law Lockhart to read to him. Lockhart, thinking of the many books that Sir Walter had written and of the great library at Abbotsford, lined from floor to ceiling with thousands of books, asked, "From what book shall I read?" And Scott answered, "Need you ask? There is but one." At the moment of the twilight of life and the dawn of eternity there was only one possible book.

One of the most famous Bible stories in the world is the story of Tockichi Ishii. Ishii was a Japanese criminal with a unique record of savage murder. He was a man of fiendish brutality, pitiless as a tiger. He had callously murdered men and women and even little children. He was captured and condemned, and he was in prison awaiting execution. He was visited by two Canadian women. They could make no impression on him; he would not even speak or answer; he simply glowered at them like a wild beast. In the end they had to go, but they left a Bible with him. For some reason Ishii began to read the book, and, when he started, he could not stop. He read on until he came to the story of the Cross. It was the saying of Jesus: "Father, forgive them; they know not what they do," that broke him. "I stopped," he said. "I was stabbed to the heart, as if pierced by a five-inch nail. Shall I call it the love of Christ? Shall I call it his compassion? I do not know what to call it. I only know that I believed, and the hardness of my heart was changed." When in the end the jailer came to lead him to the scaffold, instead of the surly, hardened, brutal, almost beastlike man he once had been, he went to death with a serene, smiling, gentle radiance, for Tockichi Ishii the murderer had been reborn by reading the word of God.

Events like these leave us in no doubt that this book is unique. We describe that uniqueness by saying that this book is inspired, that it is the word of God. But what do we mean by that?

The answer has sometimes been given that this book was written by God; that every word and syllable and letter, every page and paragraph and sentence is the writing of God; that the book is the verbatim work of God. That view is the basis of what is called verbal inspiration. As a theory of inspiration it goes very far back. On this theory the men who wrote the Bible had no more to do with what they were writing than the pen in an author's hand or the typewriter on which this chapter is being typed. In Whittingham's New Testament, the precursor of the famous Geneva Bible, the name of Paul is—rightly—not attached to the Letter to the Hebrews, and there is a note to point out that "seeing the Spirit of God is the author thereof, it diminishes nothing the authority, although we know not with what pen he wrote." The author, whoever he was, was on this view, no more than a pen in the hand of God.

Athenagoras wrote of "God moving the mouths of the prophets like musical instruments." He spoke of the Spirit using the writers as a flute-player breathes into a flute (*Embassy,* 7 B, 9 D). Justin Martyr speaks of the Divine Spirit coming down from heaven, and using men as a plectrum sweeps across a harp or lyre (*The Exhortation to the Gentiles,* 8). Theophilus of Antioch speaks of the prophets "who became the instruments of God" (*To Autolycus,* 2.9). Clement of Alexandria speaks of the sacred writers as becoming "the organs of the divine voice" (*Stromateis,* 6.18). Macarius said that, just as the breath speaks by blowing through a flute, "so the Holy Spirit spoke through holy and Spirit-bearing men" (*Homilies,* 47.14). On this view the men who wrote the books of Scripture had no more to do with what they wrote than a pen has to do with an author's book or a musical instrument has to do with a musician's music. All this would mean that the Bible is literally and, as it were, physically, the word of God. For a variety of reasons it is not possible to hold this view.

1. There is first of all this simple fact. The early manuscripts were all copied by hand, and in the copying changes and errors crept in. It has been calculated that in the Greek manuscripts of

the new Testament there are 150,000 places in which there are variant readings. True, sometimes it is only a difference in spelling or a difference in the order of the words or the substitute of one synonym for another. True, of the 150,000 fewer than 400 affect the sense, fewer than 50 are of any importance, and there is no case in which an article of faith or a precept of duty is left in doubt. This is perfectly true, but a reader would still have to decide which of the spellings, which of the variants is the word of God in the literal sense of the term. It might be said that what was the word of God was the first original manuscript as it left the hand of the original writer. If so, it is lost and gone forever.

Take the case of the English text. In the late nineteenth century a committee of the American Bible Society examined six different editions of the Authorized Version, and they found nearly 24,000 differences. True, the variations made no material difference; but if a book is verbatim the word of God, then the words must be fixed, as well as the meaning, and in the case of the Bible this is simply not so. It would have been a strange thing for God to dictate the original work and then not to take equal care for its infallible transmission.

2. There is the further fact that, whatever the biblical writers were, they were far more than pens in the hand of God, or instruments through which the Holy Spirit breathed. If this had been the case, we would have expected the Bible to be written in one level style the same all over. In point of fact every writer in the New Testament writes in his own style. If one who knows Greek well is confronted with a passage taken at random from the New Testament, and he is asked to identify the writer, even if he does not know the passage, he will have no difficulty in saying whether it was written by Mark or Luke, by John or Peter, by the writer of the Letter to the Hebrews or by the John of the Revelation. In fact the John of the Revelation often writes with such defiance of the ordinary rules of grammar and syntax that his style is unmistakable. His Greek is so bad that a modern schoolboy would get into bad trouble for writing it. There is no question of the suppression of the human personality. As G. E. Ladd has so well pointed out, the Bible is the word of God, but it is quite definitely in the words of men. The personality of the writers of the books of the Bible is certainly not obliterated. A pen and a musical instrument are things, but the biblical writers never ceased to be personalities in their own right.

Their independence is seen even in the way in which they tell a story. In the case of the story of the Gerasene demoniac, Matthew takes 7 verses to tell the story (Matthew 8:28-34); Mark takes 20 verses (Mark 5:1-20); Luke takes 14 verses (Luke 8:26-39). The Gospel writers are not men who are writing to divine or any other kind of dictation. In his writing each expresses his own personality and does things in his own way.

3. Still further, there are the variations and the actual differences between Gospel and Gospel. In the first three Gospels the incident of the cleansing of the Temple comes at the end of the life of Jesus (Matthew 21:12, 13; Mark 11:15-17; Luke 18:45, 46); in the fourth Gospel it comes at the beginning of his ministry (John 2:13-17). Take the case of the different records of the same saying. It is often legitimately possible to explain differing versions of a saying of Jesus by saying that he repeated it in different versions on different occasions. But there are certain occasions which are quite definitely the same, and yet the recorded saying of Jesus, spoken on them, varies quite considerably. Take the case of the saying which comes after Caesarea Philippi and before the Transfiguration in all the first three Gospels:

> Truly, I say to you, there are some standing here who will not taste death before they see the Son of man coming in his kingdom. (Matthew 16:28)

> Truly, I say to you, there are some standing here who will not taste death, before they see the kingdom of God come with power. (Mark 9:1)

> But I tell you truly, there are some standing here who will not taste of death before they see the kingdom of God. (Luke 9:27)

Unquestionably, we have here three versions of the same saying, and if the Gospels were written by divine dictation, surely there would not have been three versions of the one saying.

Take the case of Jesus' saying about himself at his trial, the saying which made his condemnation quite certain.

> But Jesus was silent. And the high priest said to him, I adjure you by the living God, tell us if you are the Christ, the Son of God. Jesus said to him, You have said so. But I tell you, hereafter you will see the Son of man seated at the right hand of Power, and coming on the clouds of heaven. (Matthew 26:63, 64)

> But he (Jesus) was silent and made no answer. Again the high priest asked him, Are you the Christ, the Son of the Blessed? And Jesus said, I am; and you will see the Son of man sitting at the right hand of Power, and coming with clouds of heaven. (Mark 14:61, 62)

> They said, If you are the Christ tell us. But he said to them, If I tell you, you will not believe; and if I ask you, you will not answer. But from now on the Son of man shall be seated at the right hand of the power of God. And they all said, Are you the Son of God then? And he said to them, You say that I am. (Luke 22:67-70)

Here are three different versions of the same saying on the same occasion. Divine dictation would not result in that.

One of the most surprising variations in the narratives of the Gospels is that the Gospels differ in regard to the time of Jesus' crucifixion. In the first three Gospels there is little doubt that the Last Supper is the Passover Feast (Matthew 26:17-20; Mark 14:12-17; Luke 22:7-14), and that therefore Jesus was crucified *after* the Passover. In the fourth Gospel, in John, there is no doubt at all that Jesus is said to have been crucified *before* the Passover Feast, for the Jews would not enter Pilate's judgment hall, in case they might be rendered unclean and so be disqualified from sharing in the Passover, and the day of the crucifixion is repeatedly called the day of preparation for the Passover (John 18:28; 19:31, 42). Further, in Mark the hour of the crucifixion is the third hour, 9 a.m., while in John the decision to crucify Jesus is not finally taken until the sixth hour, 12 o'clock midday. It is in the last degree improbable that divine dictation would have issued in a discrepancy like that.

4. On a very rare occasion there can be more than variation, there can be error. In the story of how the disciples plucked the ears of corn in the cornfield and so broke the sabbath law, Mark makes Jesus remind the Pharisees of what David did in the days of Abiathar the high priest (Mark 2:26). Matthew and Luke both omit the name (Matthew 12:1-8; Luke 6:1-5). The priest in question was not Abiathar; he was Ahimelech (1 Samuel 21:1-6); Ahimelech was Abiathar's son (2 Samuel 8:17). The slip of a human mind is perfectly natural and completely unimportant, but such a slip is inconceivable in divine dictation.

5. There are occasions when a man who studies Scripture has to exercise a judgment and a choice as to which of two parts of Scripture he is to follow. This is specially true in regard to Paul's teaching on marriage. In 1 Corinthians 7 Paul writes of marriage, and he is on the whole against marriage. If people are

married, he does not want them to separate; if they are married they are to carry out to each other the duties and the obligations of marriage. But marriage for Paul, when he wrote that chapter, was a second best. It is well for a man not to touch a woman, but marriage is approved as a defense against the temptation to immorality (verses 1 and 2). It is better that people should remain unmarried. But, if they cannot exercise self-control, then they may marry, because it is better to marry than to be aflame with passion (verses 8 and 9). The whole attitude is that marriage is only justifiable when it saves a man from a worse fate! Why this attitude? Because Paul at this time was expecting the coming again of Jesus Christ at any moment, today, tomorrow, within weeks; he therefore wishes a man to have no distractions at all, and to concentrate on the coming end.

I want you to be free from anxieties. The unmarried man is anxious about the affairs of the Lord, how to please the Lord; but the married man is anxious about worldly affairs, how to please his wife, and his interests are divided. And the unmarried woman or girl is anxious about the affairs of the Lord, how to be holy in body and spirit; but the married woman is anxious about worldly affairs, how to please her husband. I say this . . . to secure your undivided devotion to the Lord. (1 Corinthians 7:32-35)

Paul wrote this about A.D. 55; he is obsessed, as was the whole church, with the idea of the coming of Christ. In view of that, marriage was a second best, one of the many things which might distract a man's attention from Christ in the brief time of waiting. But about eight years passed, and Paul wrote to the Ephesians. He knows now that he and his fellow-Christians are living in a much more permanent situation, and in a great chapter he likens marriage to the relationship between Christ and his church. A man leaves father and mother for his wife. It is "a great mystery." That is to say, it is the symbol of something splendid. Marriage is nothing less than the symbol of the relationship between Christ and his church (Ephesians 5:21-33). Now, if I am asked, What is Paul's teaching about marriage? where do I go to answer the question—1 Corinthians 7 or Ephesians 5? Surely to Ephesians 5, for any man has a right to be judged by his highest teaching. In 1 Corinthians 7 Paul actually says, "To the rest I say, not the Lord . . ." (1 Corinthians 7:12). Again he says, "I have no command of the Lord, but I give my opinion as one who by the Lord's mercy is trustworthy" (1 Corinthians 7:25). He is not writing to divine dictation here; he is giving his opinion. In the years that opinion changed, but the Christian doctrine of marriage is not in 1 Corinthians 7 but in Ephesians 5.

We have now seen enough to realize that the conception of inspiration as producing a divinely dictated, infallible book produces far more problems than it solves. We must set out on some other course, and start all over again.

1. If the Bible is the word of God, it must mean that in some way in the Bible a special connection is established between God and man. In some way in the Bible God and man meet. Man who is characteristically the seeker, and God who is characteristically the revealer, come together in this book. The Bible is uniquely the meeting place of the Spirit of God and the spirit of man. That is the first essential basis of any doctrine of revelation and inspiration.

2. This means that the meaning of inspiration is to be found in the human situation, or, rather in the divine-human situation. It is in the connection established between the Spirit of God and the mind of man that the meaning of inspiration is to be found.

3. So we have to ask, What *is* the human situation? The human situation has two elements in it. The first element is that man is the creation of God; but not only the creation of God; he is also made in the image of God (Genesis 1:27). This ought to mean, as Suzanne de Dietrich puts it, that "it is the vocation of man to live in a trustful relationship with God." To put it in another way, God is not only Creator; he is also Father. But now comes the second element in this human situation. It is essential for this situation that man must be born free. The relationship between man and God must be the product of a free invitation and a free response. To quote Suzanne de Dietrich again: "Man alone in all the creation can say 'yes' or 'no' to God." In point of fact, man has said no. He uses his independence to take his own way. This is the very essence of the story of the Fall. He fails to see that his only real freedom, his only real self-fulfillment, must come from obedience to God. So man arrives at a situation in which he is traveling in the wrong direction, searching for happiness in the wrong place, looking for freedom where there is no freedom, and searching for fulfillment where there is no

fulfillment. This is sin. The human situation is a situation in which man turns away from God to himself.

4. Because God is love, God has somehow or other to mend this situation. He cannot mend it by intervention from outside; he cannot intervene directly. This is so because the relationship between man and God must remain a free and spontaneous relationship, or it cannot be a relationship of love. It is therefore necessary that God should mend the human situation by human instruments. This is what he did—and the instruments he used to recall men to himself were the prophets.

Two things are to be remembered. A prophet was not so much a *foreteller* of the future as a *forthteller* of the will and purpose of God. The great function of prophecy is not prediction; it is the proclamation of the will of God, and the announcement of the consequences, if the will of God is not obeyed. Further, prophecy was a much wider word for the Jew than it is for us. As we saw, when we were studying the making of the Old Testament, the historical books were called the former prophets; so history is prophetic. Moses was reckoned as a prophet; so law is prophetic. All Scripture is prophetic, for the prophet is the man who brings to his fellow men the voice of God. Now this is to say that the prophet is characteristically the link between God and man. This is his function; this is the reason for his existence. And, if the prophet is the man who establishes and restores the relationship between God and man, this is to say that the prophet *is* the man who speaks the word of God; the prophet *is* the inspired man.

5. If this is so, we will have gone a long way to understanding the meaning of inspiration, the meaning of the idea of the word of God, if we can understand just what a prophet is. Suzanne de Dietrich points out two characteristics of the prophet.

(a) The prophet is the conscience of the nation. He is "the living conscience of the people at a moment when all other voices are silent."

(b) The prophet is under the absolute control of God.

> The lion has roared;
> who will not fear?
> The Lord God has spoken;
> who can but prophesy? (Amos 3:8)

The prophet is the man who speaks because he must.

(c) The prophet is the man who in a special way has been in

the inner council of God. "Surely the Lord God does nothing, without revealing his secret to his servants the prophets" (Amos 3:7). The prophet is not expressing an opinion or making a suggestion. The characteristic saying of the prophet is not, "I say," but, "Thus says the Lord." So, as Wheeler Robinson said, this is the difference between the Greek and the Hebrew. For the Greek truth is something which is discovered by the searching mind of man; for the Hebrew truth is something which is revealed by the Spirit of God. The typical Hebrew statement is, "He has *showed* you, O man, what is good" (Micah 6:8). Not, "You have been able to discover what is good," but, "God has shown you what is good." The prophet is therefore quite clearly a man who must listen before he speaks. The prophet is the man who listens, who understands, and who communicates. The prophet has only one function—to restore, to establish, to maintain, to develop the relationship between God and man. He is neither scientist nor historian. His whole function has to do with the relationship between God and man.

6. We can now put this in another way—clearly the prophet must be the man who knows God. Otherwise he cannot even begin to be a prophet. When the church in which he was an elder was looking for a minister, Thomas Carlyle's father said, "What this church needs is a man who knows God other than at secondhand." The prophet knows God at firsthand.

7. But immediately the question arises—What does it mean to know? First of all, there is all the difference between *knowing about* a person and *knowing* him. There are many great figures in the political and the social and the academic and the sporting world whom we know about, although we do not actually know them at all. But still further, the word *know* is a wide-stretching word. We know many people; we know their face, their voice, their name, their job, their life story. We speak to them when we meet them; we pass the time of day with them. But how many people do we really *know?* How many people are there into whose mind and heart we can enter with sympathy and understanding, so that we know what they are thinking and feeling? That kind of knowledge depends on one further thing—it depends on love. For true knowledge there must be love. The prophet who is to bring the message of God must not only know God, he must also love God.

8. But we must take a further step. To love is necessarily to obey. The proof of love is obedience. "You are my friends,"

Jesus said, "if you do what I command you" (John 15:14). Therefore the prophet is the man who obeys God. There is a moral element in inspiration. Those who see God are pure in heart (Matthew 5:8). The man who receives the blessing has clean hands and a pure heart (Psalm 24:4, 5).

We are now coming near a definition, which takes us halfway to our goal.

An inspired book, a book which is the word of God, is a book which effects a connection between God and man, thereby correcting the human situation, which has gone wrong. It is written by a man who knows God, because he loves God, and whose love has issued in an obedience which fits him to be the instrument of God.

But we have not yet finished, because there is another line which joins up with this one. For a Jew the revelation of God was not a revelation in words at all; it was a revelation in events. For a Jew the great revelation of God is the history of Israel, and especially the deliverance from Egypt. It is in history, it is in events, it is in divine action that God reveals himself. Anyone who reads the prophets must see that a very large part of the words of the prophets consists in the interpretation of historical events. The prophet sees God's hand revealed in the event; he sees in the event what God has done, and what God is meaning to say.

We can therefore say with complete certainty that the revelation which God gives is given in action and in event; and that the Bible is rather the record and the interpretation of these events than revelation in itself. The Bible is the story of God acting and men interpreting, or failing to interpret, the action of God. And now we come to the peak of the whole matter.

The supreme event is Jesus Christ. It is he who is the Word. The word is no written page. God's words are events; God speaks in events. And therefore the supreme event, the supreme revelation, the supreme word is Jesus Christ.

The Bible tells of the *preparation* for his coming in the Old Testament; it tells of the *event* of his coming in the Gospels; it tells of the *result* of his coming in the Acts; it tells of the *interpretations* of his coming in the Letters. The correct way to read the Bible is to begin in the middle with the saving event

Jesus Christ; then to go back to the preparation, and then on to the story of the church, and the interpretations of him.

The supreme importance of the Bible is that in it and nowhere else we find Jesus Christ. Without it we would have no record of either the life or the teaching of Jesus. It may be claimed that even without the Bible we would have the tradition of the church; but it is the Bible which prevents the distortion of that tradition. It is the touchstone; it is the assurance that no man can pervert the facts or invent new facts, for Jesus Christ is there.

I believe that the Bible is the word of God because in it alone we confront him who was uniquely the Word of God. So we come back to the great Reformation principle, the word of Luther: "The true touchstone for testing any book is to discover whether it emphasizes the prominence of Christ or not. . . . What does not teach Christ is not apostolic, not even if taught by Peter or Paul. On the other hand what does preach Christ is apostolic, even if it should come from Judas, Annas, Herod, or Pilate."

Here is the simple test—the Bible is the word of God because through it we find Jesus Christ. So then finally we may sum up our conclusions:

1. The Bible is the word of God, because it is the place where the broken relationship between man and God is repaired.
2. The Bible is the word of God, because it was written by men who knew God, because they loved him and obeyed him.
3. The Bible is the word of God, because it tells of the self-revealing, saving acts of God, culminating in the event of Jesus Christ.
4. The Bible is the word of God because in it and in it alone we are confronted with the life and teaching of Jesus Christ.

Aids to Reading

(Books for further study)

The following series of commentaries will be found useful. In each of them there is a volume or part-volume on each Bible book.

Clarke's Commentary (Abingdon). This commentary covers the entire Bible. Although it is one of the older commentaries, it still remains helpful.

Interpreter's Bible (Abingdon). This is a complete and scholarly commentary on the whole Bible. It is consistently valuable.

Of the one-volume commentaries the best known of the older ones is the commentary of A. S. Peake. This *Commentary on the Bible* (Nelson) was fairly recently revised and rewritten. One of the newest of these commentaries is *The Interpreter's One-Volume Commentary on the Bible* (Abingdon). It should be remembered that one-volume commentaries are necessarily brief in their comments.

There are two older books on the Bible which are still of the greatest use. The first is *The Bible: Its Origin, Its Significance, and Its Abiding Worth* by A. S. Peake, and *A Guide to Understanding the Bible* by H. E. Fosdick (Harper). No better books on the Bible have ever been published. One of the most useful and significant of recent books is G. E. Ladd's *The New Testament and Criticism* (Eerdmans). Whatever else is read, these books should not be missed.

Of books on the background of the Bible, the *Cambridge History of the Bible;* the *Oxford Bible Atlas,* ed. Herbert G. May and G. H. Hunt; and the *Westminster Historical Atlas to the Bible,* ed. George G. Wright and F. V. Filson; are worth noting.

Two useful aids are *Eerdman's Handbook to the Bible* by David Alexander and Patricia Alexander, and the *Abingdon Bible Handbook* by Edward P. Blair.

Finally, a book to lead us back again to the Bible itself: A. E. Harvey, *The New English Bible, Companion to the New Testament* (Oxford).

FESTIVAL BOOKS—a mass-market paperback line featuring some of the finest in inspirational and theological reading. Here are just a few titles from this outstanding line:

Abundant Living by Stanley Jones $1.95   0-687-00689-9
Bless This Mess and Other Prayers by Jo Carr and Imogene Sorley $1.50   0-687-03618-6
The Divine Yes by E. Stanley Jones $1.50   0-687-10989-2
How Came the Bible? by Edgar J. Goodspeed $1.75   0-687-17524-0
Letters to Karen by Charlie W. Shedd $1.25   0-687-21566-8
The Master's Men by William Barclay $1.50   0-687-23732-7
Steps to Prayer Power by Jo Kimmel $1.50   0-687-39340-X
Strange Facts About the Bible by Webb Garrison $2.25   0-687-39945-9
Twelve Baskets of Crumbs by Elisabeth Elliot $1.75   0-687-42702-9
The Will of God by Leslie D. Weatherhead $1.25   0-687-45600-2

Buy them at your local bookstore or use this coupon for ordering.
Customer Service Manager ● Abingdon ● 201 Eighth Ave. S. ● Nashville, TN 37202
Please send the Festival books I have checked above. I am enclosing $_____ (plus 35¢ to cover postage and handling). Send check or money order. No cash or C.O.D.s please.
—Please send me a free brochure listing the complete line of Festival Books.

Name _____

Address _____

City _____ State _____ Zip _____
*Please allow three weeks for delivery